Self-Help and Personal Development

Er. Prashant Kumar Sahoo

Published by Er. Prashant Kumar Sahoo, 2024.

ISBN-: 978-93-341-2429-3

Printed in the United States of America

Table of Contents

Self-Help and Personal Development 1
Preface 2
Chapter 1: Building Self-Awareness 4
Chapter 2: Overcoming Limiting Beliefs 7
Chapter 3: Goal Setting and Achievement 10
Chapter 4: Time Management and Productivity 13
Chapter 5: Overcoming Procrastination 16
Chapter 6: Mindfulness and Stress Reduction 19
Chapter 7: Developing Emotional Intelligence 22
Chapter 8: Building Resilience 25
Chapter 9: Enhancing Self-Confidence 28
Chapter 10: Cultivating Positive Relationships 32
Chapter 11: Mastering Communication Skills 35
Chapter 12: Unlocking Creativity and Innovation 38
Chapter 13: Creating a Balanced Life 41
Chapter 14: Physical Health and Wellness 44
Chapter 15: Financial Well-being 47
Chapter 16: Digital Detox and Tech Management 50

A Heartfelt Thank You

To my dearest parents,

As I pen the final words of this book, I find myself reflecting on the journey that brought me here. It is with profound gratitude and deep appreciation that I dedicate this work to you. Your unwavering love and support have been the bedrock of my inspiration and the driving force behind every page I've written.

From my earliest days, your belief in me has been a constant source of strength and encouragement. Your sacrifices, guidance, and boundless patience have shaped not only my character but also my aspirations. It is because of your endless faith in my potential that I dared to dream, to write, and to share my thoughts with the world.

Your love has been my greatest inspiration, and your support has provided the courage I needed to pursue my passions. Every milestone I achieve, every word I write, carries a piece of your love and dedication. This book is as much a reflection of your influence as it is of my own journey.

Thank you for being my cheerleaders, my mentors, and my greatest supporters. Your role in my life is immeasurable, and I am forever grateful for the countless ways you have enriched my life. As I embark on new endeavors, I carry your wisdom and love with me, always.

With all my love and gratitude,

Er. Prashant Kumar Sahoo

Preface

In a world that moves at breakneck speed, where demands and distractions constantly pull us in every direction, it's easy to lose sight of what truly matters. We often find ourselves overwhelmed, disconnected, and searching for meaning in the noise of daily life. Yet, within each of us lies the potential for extraordinary growth, fulfillment, and transformation—if only we know how to unlock it.

This book, ***Self-Help and Personal Development*** , is a guide to that very journey. It was born out of a deep desire to help others navigate the complexities of modern life with clarity, purpose, and resilience. Each chapter represents a facet of personal growth that, when embraced, can lead to a more balanced, empowered, and joyful existence.

As you turn these pages, you'll embark on a path of self-discovery that will challenge you to look inward, set meaningful goals, and cultivate the habits and mindset needed to achieve them. You'll learn how to overcome obstacles, build stronger relationships, and tap into the creative potential that resides within you. More importantly, you'll uncover the tools to create a life that not only meets your ambitions but also nourishes your soul.

This book is more than just a collection of strategies—it's an invitation to transform your life. Whether you're just beginning your journey of personal growth or seeking to deepen the progress you've already made, you'll find insights and practical guidance here that can make a real difference.

My hope is that ***Self-Help and Personal Development*** becomes a trusted companion on your journey—a source of inspiration, encouragement, and wisdom that you can return to time and again. The path to personal mastery is not always easy, but it is immensely rewarding. I invite you to embrace the process, to challenge yourself, and to step into the life you've always dreamed of.

Thank you for allowing me to be a part of your journey. Now, let's begin.

A Note to the Reader

Imagine a life where every goal you set is within your reach, where challenges are met with resilience, and where each day brings a deeper sense of fulfillment. This book is your guide to that life. Inside these pages, you'll discover the tools and insights to unlock your true potential, to break free from the limitations that have held you back, and to create a life of purpose, balance, and joy.

Whether you're seeking to boost your confidence, master your time, or forge stronger relationships, this book offers practical strategies and timeless wisdom to help you achieve your dreams. Each chapter is a step on a transformative journey—a journey that will empower you to take control of your destiny and live the life you've always envisioned.

Are you ready to embark on this adventure of self-discovery and personal growth? Dive in, and let the journey begin. The life you've always dreamed of is just a page away.

Chapter 1: Building Self-Awareness

Building Self-Awareness: The Foundation of Personal Growth

Introduction:

Self-awareness is the cornerstone of personal growth and development. It is the ability to see yourself clearly, understand your emotions, thoughts, and behaviors, and recognize how they align with your values and impact your life. By cultivating self-awareness, you embark on a journey of discovery that leads to greater fulfillment, improved relationships, and a more purposeful life. This chapter explores the concept of self-awareness, its importance, and practical strategies to enhance your understanding of yourself.

Understanding Self-Awareness:

1. Defining Self-Awareness

Self-awareness is the conscious knowledge of your own character, emotions, desires, and motivations. It is the capacity to reflect on your inner world and understand how it influences your interactions with others and your response to external circumstances.

2. Types of Self-Awareness

Internal Self-Awareness: This refers to how clearly you understand your internal self—your emotions, beliefs, values, and how they influence your actions. It involves recognizing your strengths, weaknesses, and the impact of your thoughts and feelings on your behavior.

External Self-Awareness: This is the ability to understand how others perceive you. It involves recognizing the impact of your actions, words, and behaviors on others and adjusting them to align with your intentions.

3. The Benefits of Self-Awareness

Improved Emotional Regulation: Understanding your emotions allows you to manage them effectively, reducing impulsivity and enhancing emotional stability.

Better Decision-Making: Self-awareness helps you make decisions aligned with your values and long-term goals, leading to more satisfying outcomes.

Enhanced Relationships: By understanding yourself, you can communicate more effectively and empathize with others, leading to healthier and more meaningful relationships.

Personal Growth: Self-awareness fosters continuous self-improvement by highlighting areas for growth and encouraging lifelong learning.

Strategies for Building Self-Awareness

1. Practice Mindfulness

Mindful Observation: Pay attention to your thoughts, emotions, and physical sensations without judgment. Mindfulness helps you become more aware of your inner experiences and how they influence your behavior.

Daily Reflection: Set aside time each day to reflect on your experiences, emotions, and reactions. Journaling can be a helpful tool for capturing your thoughts and identifying patterns over time.

2. Seek Feedback

Ask for Honest Feedback: Invite feedback from trusted friends, family members, or colleagues. Understanding how others perceive you can provide valuable insights into your behavior and help you identify blind spots.

Be Open to Criticism: Embrace constructive criticism as an opportunity for growth. Consider the feedback thoughtfully and use it to make positive changes in your life.

3. Engage in Self-Reflection

Ask Thought-Provoking Questions: Regularly ask yourself questions that encourage deep reflection, such as "What are my core values?" or "How do my actions align with my goals?" These questions can help you gain clarity about your beliefs and behaviors.

Review Past Experiences: Reflect on past experiences, particularly challenging ones, to understand how they shaped your beliefs and behavior. Consider how you have grown from these experiences and what you have learned about yourself.

4. Identify Your Values

Clarify Core Values: Identify the values that are most important to you. Understanding your core values helps you make decisions and set goals that are aligned with your true self.

Align Actions with Values: Regularly assess whether your actions align with your values. When your behavior reflects your core beliefs, you experience greater integrity and satisfaction.

5. Monitor Your Emotional Responses

Track Your Emotions: Keep a journal or use an app to track your emotions throughout the day. Monitoring your emotional responses helps you identify triggers and patterns, allowing you to manage your emotions more effectively.

Analyze Emotional Triggers: When you experience strong emotions, take time to analyze the underlying causes. Understanding what triggers your emotions can help you develop strategies for managing them.

6. Develop Empathy

Practice Active Listening: Listen to others with the intention of understanding their perspectives and emotions. Empathy helps you connect with others and enhances your external self-awareness.

Consider Other Perspectives: Regularly put yourself in others' shoes to understand how your actions and words might be perceived. This practice helps you adjust your behavior to be more considerate and effective in your interactions.

7. Cultivate a Growth Mindset

Embrace Challenges: View challenges as opportunities for growth rather than obstacles. A growth mindset encourages continuous learning and self-improvement, leading to greater self-awareness.

Learn from Mistakes: Reflect on your mistakes as learning experiences. Understanding what went wrong and why helps you make better choices in the future.

8. Engage in Personal Development

Read Self-Development Books: Explore books on personal growth, psychology, and self-awareness. These resources can provide valuable insights and strategies for enhancing self-awareness.

Participate in Workshops or Seminars: Attend workshops, seminars, or courses focused on self-awareness and personal development. Engaging in structured learning environments can accelerate your self-discovery process.

Overcoming Challenges in Building Self-Awareness

1. Addressing Resistance

Acknowledge Discomfort: Building self-awareness can be uncomfortable, as it often involves confronting aspects of yourself that you may prefer to avoid. Acknowledge this discomfort and approach it with curiosity rather than resistance.

Practice Self-Compassion: Be kind to yourself as you explore your thoughts and emotions. Self-compassion helps you navigate the challenges of self-discovery without harsh self-judgment.

2. Dealing with Cognitive Biases

Recognize Biases: Be aware of cognitive biases, such as confirmation bias (favoring information that confirms your existing beliefs) or the self-serving bias (attributing successes to internal factors and failures to external factors). Recognizing these biases helps you gain a more accurate understanding of yourself.

-Challenge Assumptions: Regularly challenge your assumptions and beliefs. Consider alternative perspectives and seek evidence that contradicts your current views to gain a more balanced understanding.

3. Balancing Internal and External Awareness

Integrate Internal and External Feedback: Strive to balance your understanding of your internal world with how others perceive you. Both internal reflection and external feedback are crucial for developing a comprehensive self-awareness.

Avoid Over-Reliance on External Validation: While feedback is valuable, avoid becoming overly reliant on external validation. Trust your inner judgment and maintain a sense of self grounded in your own values and beliefs.

The Role of Self-Awareness in Personal Growth

1. Facilitating Personal Development

Goal Setting: Self-awareness enables you to set goals that align with your true desires and values, increasing your motivation and likelihood of achieving them.

Behavioral Change: By understanding the underlying motivations and triggers for your behaviors, you can make intentional changes that support your personal growth.

2. Enhancing Relationships

Improved Communication: Self-awareness helps you communicate more effectively by expressing your needs and emotions clearly and understanding others' perspectives.

Conflict Resolution: Understanding your emotional triggers and biases enables you to approach conflicts with greater empathy and objectivity, leading to more constructive resolutions.

3. Achieving Emotional Intelligence

Emotional Regulation: Self-awareness is a key component of emotional intelligence, allowing you to recognize and manage your emotions effectively.

Social Awareness: By understanding your emotions and behaviors, you can better navigate social situations and build stronger, more meaningful connections with others.

Conclusion:

Building self-awareness is a lifelong journey that opens the door to greater self-understanding, personal growth, and fulfillment. By practicing mindfulness, seeking feedback, engaging in self-reflection, and cultivating empathy, you can deepen your awareness of your internal and external worlds. Overcoming the challenges of self-discovery requires patience, self-compassion, and a commitment to continuous learning.

Embrace self-awareness as a powerful tool for living a more authentic and intentional life. As you grow in your understanding of yourself, you will find greater clarity in your decisions, more meaningful relationships, and a deeper sense of purpose. Through self-awareness, you unlock the potential to become the best version of yourself, creating a life that reflects your true values and aspirations.

Chapter 2: Overcoming Limiting Beliefs

Overcoming Limiting Beliefs: Techniques for Unlocking Your True Potential

Introduction:

Limiting beliefs are the invisible barriers that hold us back from achieving our full potential. These beliefs, often deeply ingrained in our subconscious, shape the way we view ourselves, our abilities, and the world around us. They are the silent saboteurs that keep us from pursuing our dreams, taking risks, and living a life of fulfillment. But the good news is that limiting beliefs can be identified, challenged, and ultimately transformed. This chapter will guide you through powerful techniques to overcome limiting beliefs, empowering you to step into your true potential and create the life you desire.

Understanding Limiting Beliefs

A limiting belief is a thought or idea that you accept as true, but which actually restricts your growth and potential. These beliefs often stem from past experiences, societal conditioning, or negative self-talk. They can manifest in various forms, such as:

- **I'm not good enough.**
- **I don't deserve success.**
- **I can't change.**
- **It's too late for me.**

These beliefs act as self-imposed limitations, creating a mental ceiling that keeps you from reaching higher. The first step to overcoming limiting beliefs is to become aware of them and understand how they influence your thoughts, emotions, and actions.

Identifying Your Limiting Beliefs

Before you can change a limiting belief, you must first identify it. Here are some techniques to help you uncover your limiting beliefs:

1. Self-Reflection

- Take time to reflect on areas of your life where you feel stuck or dissatisfied. Ask yourself what thoughts or beliefs might be holding you back. Pay attention to recurring patterns of negative thinking or self-doubt.

2. Journaling

- Journaling is a powerful tool for self-discovery. Write down your thoughts, fears, and challenges. As you review your entries, look for common themes or statements that indicate limiting beliefs. For example, if you often write, "I can't do this," it may reveal a belief that you're incapable of achieving your goals.

3. Mindfulness and Meditation

- Mindfulness and meditation practices can help you become more aware of your thoughts and beliefs. By observing your mind without judgment, you can notice the limiting beliefs that arise. This awareness is the first step toward change.

4. Feedback from Others

- Sometimes, others can see our limiting beliefs more clearly than we can. Ask trusted friends, family members, or mentors for feedback on your behavior or mindset. They may help you identify beliefs that you didn't realize were holding you back.

Techniques for Overcoming Limiting Beliefs

Once you've identified your limiting beliefs, it's time to challenge and reframe them. The following techniques can help you break free from these mental constraints and replace them with empowering beliefs:

1. Questioning the Belief

- One of the most effective ways to challenge a limiting belief is to question its validity. Ask yourself:

- Is this belief true?

- What evidence do I have to support this belief?

- What evidence do I have that contradicts this belief?

- How did this belief originate, and is it still relevant?

- By scrutinizing the belief, you may discover that it is based on faulty assumptions or outdated information.

2. Affirmations

- Affirmations are positive statements that you repeat to yourself to reinforce new, empowering beliefs. Create affirmations that counteract your limiting beliefs. For example, if you struggle with the belief "I'm not good enough," you could use affirmations like "I am worthy of success" or "I have the skills and abilities to achieve my goals." Repeat these affirmations daily, especially when you notice the limiting belief surfacing.

3. Visualization

- Visualization is a powerful technique for reprogramming your mind. Close your eyes and imagine yourself living a life free from limiting beliefs. Visualize yourself achieving your goals, feeling confident, and overcoming challenges with ease. The more vividly you can imagine this reality, the more your mind will begin to accept it as possible.

4. Cognitive Restructuring

- Cognitive restructuring is a process used in cognitive-behavioral therapy (CBT) to challenge and change negative thought patterns. Start by identifying a limiting belief and then write down the thoughts associated with it. Next, replace these thoughts with more balanced, realistic ones. For example, replace "I always fail" with "I have faced challenges, but I've also achieved success." This process helps you create new, healthier thought patterns.

5. Behavioral Experiments

- Sometimes, the best way to challenge a limiting belief is to test it in the real world. Design a small experiment to disprove your belief. For instance, if you believe "I'm not good at public speaking," sign up for a speaking opportunity in a low-pressure setting. The experience may provide evidence that contradicts your limiting belief and boosts your confidence.

6. Surround Yourself with Positive Influences

- The people you spend time with can significantly impact your beliefs. Surround yourself with positive, supportive individuals who encourage your growth and challenge your limiting beliefs. Their optimism and belief in your potential can inspire you to see yourself in a new light.

7. Reframe Past Experiences

- Limiting beliefs often stem from past experiences, particularly failures or negative events. Revisit these experiences and try to reframe them in a more positive or neutral light. For example, instead of viewing a past failure as proof of incompetence, see it as a valuable learning experience that contributed to your growth.

8. Practice Self-Compassion

- Overcoming limiting beliefs can be challenging, and it's essential to be kind to yourself throughout the process. Practice self-compassion by acknowledging that everyone has limiting beliefs and that changing them takes time. Treat yourself with the same kindness and understanding that you would offer to a friend.

Embracing Empowering Beliefs

As you work to overcome limiting beliefs, it's important to replace them with empowering beliefs that support your growth and potential. Empowering beliefs are thoughts and ideas that uplift and inspire you. They are rooted in self-confidence, possibility, and a growth mindset. Here are some examples of empowering beliefs:

- **I am capable of achieving my goals.**
- **I learn and grow from every experience.**
- **I deserve happiness and success.**
- **I am constantly improving and evolving.**

To reinforce these beliefs, integrate them into your daily life through affirmations, visualization, and positive self-talk. The more you focus on empowering beliefs, the more they will become your default mindset.

Conclusion:

Overcoming limiting beliefs is a transformative journey that opens the door to endless possibilities. By identifying, challenging, and reframing these beliefs, you can break free from the mental barriers that have held you back and step into a life of empowerment and fulfillment. Remember, the beliefs you hold shape your reality—choose beliefs that uplift, inspire, and propel you toward your dreams.

You have the power to rewrite your story, to redefine what is possible, and to create a life that reflects your true potential. Embrace the journey of overcoming limiting beliefs, and watch as your life transforms in ways you never imagined possible.

Chapter 3: Goal Setting and Achievement

Goal Setting and Achievement: A Pathway to Success

Introduction:

Goal setting is the cornerstone of achieving personal and professional success. It is the process of defining clear, measurable, and attainable objectives that guide your actions and decisions. Whether you aim to advance in your career, enhance your personal life, or pursue a new skill, effective goal setting serves as a compass that directs you toward your desired outcomes. This chapter explores the significance of goal setting, the principles behind effective goal management, and actionable strategies to help you set and achieve your goals.

The Importance of Goal Setting

1. Provides Direction and Focus

Setting goals offers a clear sense of direction. It transforms vague desires into concrete objectives, giving you a roadmap to follow. Without goals, it's easy to become overwhelmed by the demands of daily life and lose sight of your aspirations. Goals help you prioritize your efforts, align your actions with your values, and maintain focus on what truly matters.

2. Enhances Motivation

Goals serve as a powerful source of motivation. They ignite your passion and drive, encouraging you to take proactive steps toward your aspirations. When you have a clear vision of what you want to achieve, it fuels your determination and perseverance. This motivation helps you overcome obstacles, stay committed, and push through challenges.

3. Boosts Self-Esteem

Achieving goals enhances your self-esteem and confidence. Each milestone reached is a testament to your abilities and efforts. As you accomplish your objectives, you gain a sense of pride and self-worth. This positive reinforcement reinforces your belief in your capacity to achieve even greater things.

4. Facilitates Personal Growth

Goal setting is a catalyst for personal development. It encourages you to step out of your comfort zone, learn new skills, and expand your horizons. As you work towards your goals, you gain valuable experiences, insights, and competencies that contribute to your overall growth and success.

Principles of Effective Goal Setting

1. Set SMART Goals

The SMART criteria are a widely recognized framework for effective goal setting. SMART stands for Specific, Measurable, Achievable, Relevant, and Time-bound:

Specific: Clearly define what you want to achieve. A specific goal addresses the who, what, where, when, and why.

Measurable: Establish criteria for measuring progress and success. This helps you track your achievements and stay motivated.

Achievable: Ensure that your goal is realistic and attainable. It should challenge you but remain within your reach.

Relevant: Align your goal with your broader objectives and values. It should be meaningful and significant to you.

Time-bound: Set a deadline for achieving your goal. A timeframe creates a sense of urgency and helps you stay focused.

2. Break Goals into Manageable Steps

Large goals can be daunting, but breaking them into smaller, manageable steps makes them more achievable. Create an action plan that outlines the specific tasks and milestones required to reach your goal. This approach not only makes the process less overwhelming but also provides a clear path to success.

3. Prioritize Your Goals

Not all goals are equally important. Prioritize your goals based on their significance and impact. Focus on high-priority goals that align with your long-term vision and values. This ensures that your efforts are directed toward what matters most and prevents you from spreading yourself too thin.

4. Stay Flexible and Adaptable

While it's important to have a plan, be prepared to adapt and adjust your goals as needed. Life is unpredictable, and circumstances may change. Stay flexible and open to modifying your goals or action plan if necessary. Adaptability allows you to navigate obstacles and seize new opportunities that may arise.

Strategies for Achieving Your Goals

1. Visualize Success

Visualization is a powerful technique for achieving goals. Spend time imagining yourself reaching your goal and experiencing the associated success. Visualization helps reinforce your commitment, boost motivation, and create a positive mindset. It also helps you mentally prepare for the steps needed to achieve your objectives.

2. Develop a Detailed Action Plan

Create a detailed action plan that outlines the steps, resources, and timelines required to achieve your goal. Break down each task into smaller, actionable items and set deadlines for completion. A well-structured action plan keeps you organized, focused, and accountable.

3. Track Your Progress

Regularly monitor your progress to stay on track. Use tools such as journals, progress trackers, or apps to record your achievements and evaluate your performance. Tracking progress provides valuable feedback, helps you identify areas for improvement, and keeps you motivated as you see your accomplishments.

4. Seek Support and Accountability

Share your goals with supportive friends, family, or mentors who can provide encouragement and accountability. Having someone to support you and hold you accountable can increase your commitment and motivation. Consider joining a goal-setting group or finding an accountability partner to share progress and challenges.

5. Celebrate Milestones

Celebrate your achievements and milestones along the way. Recognizing and rewarding yourself for reaching specific targets reinforces positive behavior and keeps you motivated. Celebrations can be small, such as treating yourself to something you enjoy, or larger, depending on the significance of the milestone.

6. Learn from Setbacks

Setbacks and challenges are a natural part of the journey toward achieving goals. Instead of viewing them as failures, use them as opportunities to learn and grow. Analyze what went wrong, identify lessons learned, and adjust your approach accordingly. Resilience and adaptability are key to overcoming obstacles and continuing toward your goal.

7. Maintain a Positive Mindset

A positive mindset is crucial for goal achievement. Cultivate optimism and focus on solutions rather than dwelling on problems. Positive thinking helps you stay motivated, overcome self-doubt, and approach challenges with confidence. Surround yourself with positivity and practice self-compassion to maintain a constructive attitude.

The Role of Reflection and Evaluation

1. Reflect on Your Achievements

Regular reflection allows you to assess your progress, celebrate achievements, and identify areas for improvement. Take time to review your goals, evaluate what has worked well, and consider what adjustments may be needed. Reflection helps you stay aligned with your objectives and ensures that you continue to grow and develop.

2. Evaluate and Adjust Goals

Periodically evaluate your goals to ensure they remain relevant and achievable. As you progress and grow, your priorities and aspirations may evolve. Adjust your goals and action plans as needed to reflect your current situation and long-term vision. Flexibility ensures that your goals continue to align with your evolving aspirations.

Conclusion:

Goal setting and achievement are integral to personal and professional success. By setting clear, achievable goals and following a strategic approach, you can turn your aspirations into tangible results. Effective goal management involves defining SMART objectives, breaking goals into manageable steps, prioritizing tasks, and staying adaptable. With the right strategies, support, and mindset, you can navigate the path to success and achieve your dreams.

Embrace the journey of goal setting as an opportunity for growth and self-discovery. Celebrate your achievements, learn from setbacks, and continuously reflect on your progress. Remember, the pursuit of goals is not just about reaching a destination but also about the transformation and growth experienced along the way. With dedication, perseverance, and a clear vision, you can achieve greatness and live a life filled with purpose and fulfillment.

Chapter 4: Time Management and Productivity

Time Management and Productivity: Mastering the Art of Efficiency

Introduction:

In our fast-paced world, managing time effectively and enhancing productivity are crucial skills for achieving personal and professional success. Time management involves planning and exercising control over how we spend our hours, while productivity focuses on maximizing output with the resources available. Mastering both can lead to a more organized, fulfilling, and balanced life. This chapter explores the principles of time management and productivity, their importance, and practical strategies for mastering these essential skills.

Understanding Time Management

1. Defining Time Management

Time management is the process of planning and controlling how much time to spend on specific activities. Effective time management enables individuals to accomplish more in a shorter period, reduce stress, and lead a more balanced life. It involves setting priorities, making informed decisions, and allocating time effectively to achieve desired goals.

2. The Benefits of Time Management

Increased Productivity: Efficient time management helps individuals focus on high-priority tasks and complete them more effectively.

Reduced Stress: By managing time well, individuals can avoid last-minute rushes and the anxiety associated with looming deadlines.

Improved Work-Life Balance: Effective time management allows for a balanced allocation of time between work and personal life, leading to greater overall satisfaction.

Enhanced Goal Achievement: Properly managed time contributes to the achievement of short-term and long-term goals, providing a sense of accomplishment and progress.

Understanding Productivity

1. Defining Productivity

Productivity refers to the measure of efficiency in completing tasks and achieving goals. It involves maximizing output while minimizing input, including time, effort, and resources. High productivity means getting more done in less time, leading to better results and greater satisfaction.

2. The Benefits of Productivity

Achievement of Goals: Increased productivity helps individuals reach their objectives more effectively, contributing to personal and professional success.

Enhanced Efficiency: Productivity boosts efficiency by optimizing workflows, reducing wasted time, and improving overall performance.

Greater Motivation: Accomplishing tasks and achieving goals increases motivation and confidence, fostering a sense of progress and fulfillment.

Improved Quality: Efficient processes often lead to higher quality outcomes, as individuals have more time to focus on refining and improving their work.

Strategies for Effective Time Management

1. Set Clear Goals

Define Objectives: Establish specific, measurable, achievable, relevant, and time-bound (SMART) goals. Clear objectives provide direction and motivation for managing your time effectively.

Prioritize Tasks: Prioritize tasks based on their importance and urgency. Use tools like the Eisenhower Matrix to categorize tasks and focus on what truly matters.

2. Create a Schedule

Develop a Routine: Establish a daily or weekly schedule that outlines your tasks and activities. Consistent routines help manage time efficiently and ensure important tasks are completed.

Use Time Blocks: Allocate specific time blocks for different tasks or activities. Time blocking helps maintain focus and prevents multitasking, leading to more effective time management.

3. Utilize Planning Tools

Use Calendars: Keep track of deadlines, appointments, and events using physical or digital calendars. Calendars provide a visual overview of your schedule and help you stay organized.

Employ Task Lists: Create to-do lists to outline tasks and track progress. Task lists help prioritize and manage daily activities, providing a sense of accomplishment as tasks are completed.

4. Avoid Procrastination

Identify Triggers: Recognize the factors that contribute to procrastination and address them. Understanding why you procrastinate helps develop strategies to overcome it.

Use the Pomodoro Technique: Break work into short intervals (e.g., 25 minutes) followed by short breaks. This technique helps maintain focus and reduces the likelihood of procrastination.

5. Delegate and Outsource

Identify Delegable Tasks: Determine tasks that can be delegated to others or outsourced. Delegating responsibilities frees up time for higher-priority activities and enhances overall productivity.

Communicate Clearly: When delegating tasks, provide clear instructions and expectations. Effective communication ensures that tasks are completed efficiently and to your satisfaction.

6. Minimize Distractions

Create a Focused Workspace: Designate a specific area for work that is free from distractions. A well-organized and quiet workspace enhances concentration and productivity.

Limit Digital Distractions: Manage notifications and limit time spent on social media or unrelated websites. Use tools and apps to block distractions and stay focused on your tasks.

7. Practice Time Management Techniques

The 2-Minute Rule: If a task takes less than two minutes to complete, do it immediately. This technique helps manage small tasks efficiently and prevents them from piling up.

The ABC Method: Categorize tasks into three categories: A (high priority), B (medium priority), and C (low priority). Focus on completing high-priority tasks first.

Strategies for Enhancing Productivity

1. Optimize Workflow

Streamline Processes: Identify and eliminate inefficiencies in your workflow. Streamlining processes and eliminating unnecessary steps enhance overall productivity.

Use Productivity Tools: Utilize tools and apps that support productivity, such as project management software, time trackers, and automation tools.

2. Focus on One Task at a Time

Avoid Multitasking: Focus on one task at a time to improve the quality and efficiency of your work. Multitasking can reduce productivity and increase the likelihood of errors.

Use Task Prioritization: Prioritize tasks based on their importance and deadlines. Tackling high-priority tasks first ensures that critical work is completed on time.

3. Take Regular Breaks

Schedule Breaks: Incorporate regular breaks into your work schedule to rest and recharge. Short breaks help maintain focus and prevent burnout.

Engage in Relaxing Activities: Use breaks to engage in activities that promote relaxation and mental well-being, such as stretching, walking, or mindfulness exercises.

4. Maintain a Healthy Work-Life Balance

Set Boundaries: Establish clear boundaries between work and personal time. Avoid overworking and ensure that you allocate time for relaxation, hobbies, and social activities.

Prioritize Self-Care: Engage in self-care practices that support physical, emotional, and mental health. A healthy lifestyle enhances productivity and overall well-being.

5. Continuously Improve

Reflect on Performance: Regularly assess your productivity and time management practices. Reflect on what works well and identify areas for improvement.

Seek Feedback: Gather feedback from colleagues, mentors, or supervisors to gain insights into your productivity and areas for enhancement.

Time Management and Productivity in Different Contexts:

1. In the Workplace

Set Work Priorities: Clearly define work priorities and align them with organizational goals. Effective prioritization ensures that important tasks are completed efficiently.

Implement Efficiency Strategies: Apply productivity strategies such as time blocking, task delegation, and workflow optimization to enhance workplace performance.

2. In Personal Life

Manage Household Tasks: Use time management techniques to organize and complete household tasks efficiently. Create schedules and checklists to stay on top of personal responsibilities. Pursue Personal Goals: Apply productivity principles to personal projects and hobbies. Set clear goals and create action plans to achieve them effectively.

3. In Academic Settings

Create Study Schedules: Develop a study schedule that includes time for coursework, assignments, and revision. Effective scheduling helps manage academic responsibilities and reduces stress.

Use Study Techniques: Apply productivity techniques such as focused study sessions and active learning strategies to enhance academic performance.

Conclusion:

Mastering time management and productivity is a transformative journey that leads to greater efficiency, reduced stress, and enhanced satisfaction in both personal and professional life. By setting clear goals, creating effective schedules, utilizing planning tools, and optimizing workflows, you can achieve more in less time and with greater ease.

Embrace the principles of time management and productivity with intention and commitment. Reflect on your practices, seek continuous improvement, and prioritize well-being to maintain a balanced and fulfilling life. Through effective time management and productivity, you unlock your full potential, achieve your goals, and create a life of purpose and accomplishment.

Chapter 5: Overcoming Procrastination

Overcoming Procrastination: Unlocking Your Potential

Introduction:

Procrastination is a common challenge that many people face. It's the act of delaying tasks or decisions, often resulting in unnecessary stress and missed opportunities. Overcoming procrastination is essential for achieving personal and professional goals, maintaining productivity, and improving overall well-being. This chapter explores the nature of procrastination, its underlying causes, and effective strategies to overcome it. By understanding procrastination and implementing practical solutions, you can unlock your potential and achieve greater success.

Understanding Procrastination

1. Defining Procrastination

Procrastination is the tendency to put off tasks or decisions that need to be made, often opting for more enjoyable or less demanding activities instead. It is characterized by an avoidance of tasks, leading to delays, increased stress, and a backlog of responsibilities. Procrastination can affect various aspects of life, including work, studies, and personal projects.

2. The Psychology Behind Procrastination

Procrastination is not merely about poor time management; it often involves deeper psychological factors. Some common reasons for procrastination include:

Fear of Failure: The anxiety of not meeting expectations can lead to avoidance of tasks.

Perfectionism: A desire for tasks to be perfect can result in delays as individuals wait for the "right" moment or conditions.

Lack of Motivation: When tasks seem uninteresting or irrelevant, motivation to complete them diminishes.

Overwhelm: Large or complex tasks can feel daunting, leading to avoidance and procrastination.

Poor Time Management: Difficulty in organizing tasks and managing time can contribute to procrastination.

The Impact of Procrastination

1. Increased Stress and Anxiety

Procrastination often leads to increased stress and anxiety as deadlines approach and tasks accumulate. The constant worry about unfinished tasks can create a cycle of stress, further impairing productivity and well-being.

2. Decreased Productivity

Delaying tasks results in decreased productivity and efficiency. As tasks pile up, it becomes more challenging to complete them effectively, leading to a sense of stagnation and frustration.

3. Strained Relationships

Procrastination can impact relationships, especially in collaborative settings. Delays and unmet commitments can create tension and strain trust among colleagues, friends, and family members.

4. Missed Opportunities

Procrastination can result in missed opportunities, whether in career advancement, personal growth, or achieving long-term goals. Delaying action may prevent you from seizing valuable chances and realizing your full potential.

Strategies for Overcoming Procrastination

1. Set Clear and Achievable Goals

Clear and achievable goals provide direction and motivation. Break larger goals into smaller, manageable tasks with specific deadlines. This approach makes tasks less overwhelming and provides a sense of accomplishment as you complete each step.

2. Use the Pomodoro Technique

The Pomodoro Technique is a time management method that involves working in focused intervals, typically 25 minutes, followed by a short break. This technique helps maintain concentration and prevents burnout by providing regular rest periods.

3. Prioritize Tasks

Prioritizing tasks helps you focus on what is most important and urgent. Use methods such as the Eisenhower Matrix to categorize tasks into four quadrants: urgent and important, important but not urgent, urgent but not important, and neither urgent nor important. Focus on high-priority tasks to make the most significant impact.

4. Create a Structured Routine

A structured routine helps establish a consistent work pattern and reduces the likelihood of procrastination. Set specific times for work, breaks, and leisure activities to create a balanced and productive schedule.

5. Minimize Distractions

Identify and minimize distractions that may interfere with your ability to focus. This may involve creating a dedicated workspace, turning off notifications, or using apps that block distracting websites. A clutter-free and focused environment enhances productivity.

6. Practice Self-Compassion

Be kind and compassionate to yourself when facing procrastination. Avoid self-criticism and negative self-talk, which can exacerbate feelings of guilt and anxiety. Instead, recognize that procrastination is a common challenge and focus on taking positive steps forward.

7. Utilize Time Management Tools

Time management tools, such as planners, calendars, and task management apps, can help you organize tasks and stay on track. Set reminders and deadlines to keep yourself accountable and ensure timely completion of tasks.

8. Adopt a Growth Mindset

Adopting a growth mindset involves viewing challenges and setbacks as opportunities for learning and improvement. Embrace the idea that effort and perseverance lead to success, and approach tasks with a positive attitude and a willingness to grow.

9. Seek Accountability and Support

Share your goals and progress with a trusted friend, family member, or mentor who can provide encouragement and hold you accountable. Having someone to support and check in with can increase your commitment and motivation.

10. Reflect and Adjust

Regularly reflect on your progress and adjust your strategies as needed. Assess what is working well and what areas need improvement. Adapt your approach based on your experiences and feedback to continually refine your approach to overcoming procrastination.

Building Healthy Habits

1. Develop a Productive Mindset

Cultivate a productive mindset by focusing on the benefits of completing tasks and the satisfaction of achieving goals. Visualize the positive outcomes and rewards associated with finishing tasks to stay motivated.

2. Implement Positive Reinforcement

Reward yourself for completing tasks and reaching milestones. Positive reinforcement helps reinforce good habits and provides motivation to continue working toward your goals.

3. Practice Mindfulness and Stress Management

Mindfulness and stress management techniques, such as meditation, deep breathing, and exercise, can help reduce anxiety and improve focus. Incorporate these practices into your routine to enhance overall well-being and productivity.

4. Create a Positive Work Environment

A positive work environment contributes to motivation and productivity. Surround yourself with inspiring and supportive elements, such as motivational quotes, comfortable workspaces, and uplifting music.

Overcoming Procrastination in Specific Contexts

1. Academic Settings

For students, procrastination can impact academic performance. Implement study schedules, set specific goals for each study session, and use techniques like active learning and spaced repetition to enhance focus and retention.

2. Professional Environments

In the workplace, procrastination can affect career advancement and job performance. Develop clear project plans, communicate effectively with colleagues, and prioritize tasks based on deadlines and importance.

3. Personal Projects

For personal projects, such as hobbies or self-improvement, establish clear objectives and deadlines. Break projects into manageable steps and celebrate progress to stay motivated and committed.

Conclusion:

Overcoming procrastination is a journey that requires self-awareness, effective strategies, and consistent effort. By understanding the underlying causes of procrastination and implementing practical solutions, you can enhance your productivity, reduce stress, and achieve your goals. Embrace the process of change with a positive mindset and a commitment to growth. With determination and perseverance, you can break free from procrastination and unlock your full potential.

Remember, overcoming procrastination is not about achieving perfection but about making progress and taking proactive steps toward your aspirations. Celebrate your successes, learn from setbacks, and continuously strive to improve. Through dedication and self-discipline, you can transform procrastination into a catalyst for success and fulfillment.

Chapter 6: Mindfulness and Stress Reduction

Mindfulness and Stress Reduction: A Path to Inner Peace

Introduction:

In today's fast-paced world, stress has become an almost inevitable part of life. The constant demands of work, family, and personal responsibilities can create a whirlwind of anxiety and overwhelm. Amidst this chaos, mindfulness emerges as a powerful tool for stress reduction and overall well-being. This chapter explores the concept of mindfulness, its benefits for stress reduction, and practical strategies for incorporating mindfulness into daily life. By embracing mindfulness, you can cultivate inner peace, enhance emotional resilience, and achieve a more balanced and fulfilling life.

Understanding Mindfulness

1. Defining Mindfulness

Mindfulness is the practice of being fully present in the moment, aware of your thoughts, feelings, and surroundings without judgment. It involves paying attention to your experiences as they unfold, embracing each moment with openness and curiosity. Mindfulness encourages a state of conscious awareness, allowing you to observe your internal and external experiences without being overwhelmed or reactive.

2. The Origins of Mindfulness Mindfulness has its roots in ancient contemplative traditions, particularly within Buddhism. It has been practiced for centuries as a means of cultivating awareness and inner peace. In recent years, mindfulness has gained widespread recognition and popularity in the West due to its evidence-based benefits for mental health and well-being.

3. The Principles of Mindfulness

Mindfulness is guided by several key principles:

Presence: Being fully engaged in the present moment, rather than dwelling on the past or worrying about the future.

Non-Judgment: Observing thoughts and feelings without labeling them as good or bad. Embracing experiences with an open and accepting attitude.

Acceptance: Acknowledging and accepting your emotions and experiences without resistance or avoidance.

Awareness: Developing a heightened awareness of your thoughts, feelings, and bodily sensations.

The Benefits of Mindfulness for Stress Reduction

1. Reduces Stress and Anxiety

Mindfulness helps reduce stress and anxiety by promoting relaxation and emotional regulation. By focusing on the present moment, you can break free from cycles of rumination and worry. Mindfulness practices such as meditation and deep breathing activate the body's relaxation response, reducing the physical and psychological effects of stress.

2. Enhances Emotional Regulation

Mindfulness enhances your ability to regulate emotions by fostering a greater understanding of your emotional responses. Through mindful awareness, you can identify and acknowledge your emotions without being overwhelmed by them. This awareness allows you to respond to emotions in a more balanced and constructive manner.

3. Improves Focus and Concentration

Practicing mindfulness improves focus and concentration by training the mind to stay present and attentive. Mindfulness exercises help you develop greater cognitive control, reducing distractions and enhancing your ability to concentrate on tasks. Improved focus contributes to better productivity and reduced stress.

4. Promotes Overall Well-Being

Mindfulness contributes to overall well-being by fostering a positive outlook and enhancing self-awareness. By cultivating a mindful attitude, you can develop a greater sense of gratitude, contentment, and inner peace. Mindfulness practices also support physical health by promoting relaxation and reducing stress-related ailments.

Practical Strategies for Incorporating Mindfulness into Daily Life

1. Mindful Breathing

-Mindful breathing involves paying attention to your breath and using it as an anchor to the present moment. To practice mindful breathing:

- Find a comfortable seated position with your back straight.
- Close your eyes and take a deep breath in through your nose, allowing your abdomen to rise.
- Exhale slowly through your mouth, letting go of any tension.
- Focus your attention on the sensation of your breath as it enters and leaves your body.
- Continue to breathe mindfully for a few minutes, gently bringing your attention back to your breath if your mind wanders.

2. Body Scan Meditation

Body scan meditation involves directing your attention to different parts of your body to increase awareness and release tension. To practice a body scan:

- Lie down or sit comfortably with your eyes closed.
- Begin by focusing on your toes and gradually move your attention upward through your body.
- Notice any sensations, such as warmth, tension, or relaxation, without judgment.
- Take a moment to breathe into any areas of tension, allowing them to release.
- Continue scanning through your body until you reach the top of your head.

3. Mindful Eating

Mindful eating involves paying full attention to the experience of eating and drinking. To practice mindful eating:

- Choose a meal or snack to eat mindfully.
- Sit down at a table and take a moment to appreciate the appearance, aroma, and texture of your food.
- Take small bites and chew slowly, savoring the flavors and sensations.
- Notice the feeling of hunger and fullness, and eat until you are comfortably satisfied.
- Avoid distractions such as television or smart phones while eating.

4. Mindful Walking

Mindful walking involves paying attention to the experience of walking and being present with each step. To practice mindful walking:

- Choose a quiet and safe space to walk, such as a park or a calm street.
- Walk at a comfortable pace, focusing on the sensation of each step.
- Notice the feeling of your feet touching the ground, the movement of your legs, and the rhythm of your breath.
- Observe your surroundings with curiosity and appreciation, without getting caught up in distractions.

5. Mindfulness in Daily Activities

Incorporate mindfulness into daily activities by bringing your full attention to routine tasks. For example:

- When brushing your teeth, pay attention to the sensation of the toothbrush, the taste of the toothpaste, and the sound of brushing.
- During showering, focus on the feeling of water on your skin, the fragrance of soap, and the warmth of the water.
- While washing dishes, notice the texture of the dishes, the sensation of water, and the sound of scrubbing.

Overcoming Challenges in Mindfulness Practice

1. Dealing with a Wandering Mind

It is natural for the mind to wander during mindfulness practice. When you notice your thoughts drifting, gently bring your attention back to your chosen anchor, such as your breath or bodily sensations. Be patient with yourself and avoid self-criticism.

2. Managing Time Constraints

If you have a busy schedule, start with short mindfulness practices and gradually increase the duration as you become more comfortable. Even a few minutes of mindfulness each day can have significant benefits. Find moments throughout your day to incorporate mindfulness, such as during breaks or before bed.

3. Navigating Emotional Resistance

Mindfulness practice may bring up difficult emotions or memories. Approach these emotions with compassion and curiosity, allowing yourself to experience them without judgment. Seeking support from a therapist or mindfulness teacher can also be helpful if you encounter challenging emotions.

Integrating Mindfulness into Your Lifestyle

1. Establish a Routine

Create a regular mindfulness practice by setting aside dedicated time each day for mindfulness exercises. Consistency is key to developing and maintaining mindfulness skills. Choose a time that works best for you, whether in the morning, during a lunch break, or before bedtime.

2. Join a Mindfulness Community

Consider joining a mindfulness group or community to connect with others who share similar interests. Participating in group practices, workshops, or retreats can provide support, guidance, and motivation. Engaging with a community can also enhance your understanding and practice of mindfulness.

3. Explore Mindfulness Resources

Explore various resources such as books, apps, and online courses to deepen your mindfulness practice. Resources can provide guidance, techniques, and inspiration to enhance your practice and address specific areas of interest.

Conclusion:

Mindfulness is a powerful tool for reducing stress and enhancing overall well-being. By cultivating mindfulness, you can develop greater self-awareness, emotional resilience, and inner peace. Incorporating mindfulness into daily life through practices such as mindful breathing, body scan meditation, and mindful eating can lead to profound benefits for both mental and physical health.

Embrace mindfulness as a journey rather than a destination, and approach your practice with patience and compassion. By integrating mindfulness into your lifestyle, you can create a more balanced, fulfilling, and peaceful life. Remember, the path to inner peace is a continuous process of discovery and growth. Through the practice of mindfulness, you can navigate life's challenges with grace and clarity, fostering a deeper sense of connection and well-being.

Chapter 7: Developing Emotional Intelligence

Developing Emotional Intelligence: A Journey to Personal and Professional Growth

Introduction:

Emotional Intelligence (EI) is the ability to recognize, understand, manage, and utilize emotions effectively. It encompasses a range of skills that contribute to successful interpersonal relationships, personal well-being, and professional effectiveness. Developing emotional intelligence is a transformative process that enhances self-awareness, empathy, and communication. This chapter explores the components of emotional intelligence, its significance, and practical strategies for cultivating these skills to foster growth and success.

Understanding Emotional Intelligence

1. Defining Emotional Intelligence

Emotional Intelligence refers to the capacity to perceive, comprehend, and regulate emotions in oneself and others. It involves recognizing emotional states, understanding their impact, and using this awareness to guide behavior and interactions. Emotional intelligence is essential for navigating social complexities, building meaningful relationships, and making informed decisions.

2. Components of Emotional Intelligence

Emotional Intelligence comprises several key components:

Self-Awareness: The ability to recognize and understand your own emotions, strengths, and weaknesses. Self-awareness involves introspection and reflection on how emotions influence your thoughts and actions.

Self-Regulation: The capacity to manage and control your emotions, particularly in challenging situations. Self-regulation involves staying calm under pressure, managing stress, and adapting to changing circumstances.

Motivation: The drive to achieve goals and persist in the face of setbacks. Motivation is characterized by a strong sense of purpose, enthusiasm, and resilience.

Empathy: The ability to understand and share the feelings of others. Empathy involves recognizing emotions in others, responding with sensitivity, and building strong, supportive relationships.

Social Skills: The ability to navigate social interactions effectively, communicate clearly, and build positive relationships. Social skills include active listening, conflict resolution, and teamwork.

The Significance of Emotional Intelligence

1. Enhances Personal Well-Being

Emotional intelligence contributes to personal well-being by fostering self-awareness and self-regulation. Understanding and managing your emotions helps reduce stress, improve mental health, and enhance overall life satisfaction. Emotional intelligence also enables you to navigate challenges with resilience and maintain a positive outlook.

2. Improves Professional Effectiveness

In the workplace, emotional intelligence is crucial for effective leadership, teamwork, and communication. Leaders with high emotional intelligence inspire and motivate their teams, manage conflicts constructively, and create a positive work environment. Employees with strong EI skills collaborate effectively, handle stress, and build meaningful professional relationships.

3. Strengthens Relationships

Emotional intelligence enhances interpersonal relationships by fostering empathy, understanding, and effective communication. By recognizing and validating others' emotions, you can build trust, resolve conflicts, and create deeper, more meaningful connections. EI also helps you navigate social dynamics with sensitivity and respect.

4. Facilitates Personal Growth

Developing emotional intelligence is a pathway to personal growth and self-improvement. It encourages introspection, self-awareness, and a willingness to learn from experiences. By enhancing your emotional skills, you can achieve greater self-fulfillment, resilience, and overall life satisfaction.

Strategies for Developing Emotional Intelligence

1. Cultivate Self-Awareness

Practice Mindfulness: Engage in mindfulness practices such as meditation or deep breathing to increase awareness of your emotions and thoughts. Mindfulness helps you observe your emotional responses without judgment and gain insight into your inner experiences.

Keep a Journal: Maintain a journal to reflect on your daily emotional experiences, thoughts, and reactions. Regular journaling helps you identify patterns, triggers, and areas for improvement.

Seek Feedback: Ask for constructive feedback from trusted friends, family, or colleagues. Their perspectives can provide valuable insights into how your emotions and behavior impact others.

2. Enhance Self-Regulation

Develop Coping Strategies: Identify effective coping strategies for managing stress and emotional challenges. Techniques such as deep breathing, progressive muscle relaxation, or engaging in hobbies can help you stay calm and composed.

Set Realistic Goals: Establish realistic and achievable goals to manage your expectations and reduce feelings of frustration. Break down larger goals into smaller, manageable steps to maintain a sense of control and progress.

Practice Emotional Reframing: Learn to reframe negative thoughts and emotions by focusing on positive aspects or alternative perspectives. Reframing helps you shift your mindset and respond more constructively to challenges.

3. Foster Motivation

Set Meaningful Goals: Define clear, meaningful goals that align with your values and passions. Setting goals that resonate with your core motivations helps you stay driven and committed.

Celebrate Achievements: Recognize and celebrate your accomplishments, both big and small. Celebrating milestones reinforces positive behavior and maintains motivation.

Develop a Growth Mindset: Embrace a growth mindset by viewing challenges and setbacks as opportunities for learning and improvement. Approach obstacles with curiosity and a willingness to adapt and grow.

4. Enhance Empathy

Practice Active Listening: Engage in active listening by fully focusing on the speaker, acknowledging their emotions, and responding with empathy. Avoid interrupting or making assumptions, and ask open-ended questions to deepen your understanding.

Show Genuine Interest: Demonstrate genuine interest in others' experiences and feelings. Ask about their perspectives, validate their emotions, and offer support when needed.

Engage in Perspective-Taking: Practice perspective-taking by considering situations from others' viewpoints. This helps you understand their emotions, motivations, and challenges, fostering greater empathy and compassion.

5. Develop Social Skills

Improve Communication: Focus on clear and effective communication by expressing your thoughts and emotions openly and respectfully. Use non-verbal cues, such as eye contact and body language, to reinforce your message.

Resolve Conflicts Constructively: Approach conflicts with a problem-solving mindset, seeking mutually beneficial solutions. Use active listening, assertiveness, and empathy to address issues and maintain positive relationships.

Build Teamwork Skills: Collaborate effectively with others by valuing diverse perspectives, contributing to group goals, and supporting team members. Strong teamwork skills foster positive relationships and enhance overall group performance.

Building Emotional Intelligence in Everyday Life

1. Create a Supportive Environment

Surround yourself with supportive individuals who encourage your personal growth and development. A positive and nurturing environment fosters emotional intelligence by providing opportunities for feedback, support, and collaboration.

2. Engage in Continuous Learning

Commit to ongoing learning and self-improvement by seeking resources such as books, workshops, or courses on emotional intelligence. Continuous learning helps you refine your skills and stay informed about new techniques and insights.

3. Practice Self-Care

Prioritize self-care to maintain emotional balance and well-being. Engage in activities that promote relaxation, health, and happiness, such as exercise, hobbies, and social connections. Self-care supports emotional resilience and enhances overall emotional intelligence.

4. Reflect and Evaluate

Regularly reflect on your emotional experiences, interactions, and progress. Evaluate your growth and identify areas for further development. Reflection helps you stay mindful of your emotional journey and adjust your strategies as needed.

Conclusion:

Developing emotional intelligence is a transformative journey that enriches personal and professional aspects of life. By cultivating self-awareness, self-regulation, motivation, empathy, and social skills, you can enhance your emotional intelligence and unlock your full potential. Embrace the process with dedication and an open mind, and celebrate the progress you make along the way.

Remember, emotional intelligence is not a fixed trait but a dynamic skill set that evolves with practice and experience. By committing to continuous growth and self-improvement, you can foster deeper relationships, achieve greater success, and lead a more fulfilling and balanced life. Through the journey of developing emotional intelligence, you not only enhance your own well-being but also contribute positively to the lives of those around you.

Chapter 8: Building Resilience

Building Resilience: Strength Through Adversity

Introduction:

Resilience is the ability to bounce back from adversity, adapt to challenges, and continue growing in the face of difficulties. It is a vital quality that allows individuals to withstand and recover from life's inevitable setbacks. Building resilience is not about avoiding or denying challenges but about developing the inner strength and skills to handle them effectively. This chapter explores the concept of resilience, its importance, and practical strategies for building and nurturing this invaluable quality.

Understanding Resilience

1. Defining Resilience

Resilience is the capacity to endure and recover from difficulties, trauma, or stress. It involves maintaining a sense of balance and perspective despite facing adversity. Resilient individuals possess the ability to adapt to changing circumstances, learn from challenges, and emerge stronger from their experiences.

2. The Foundations of Resilience

Resilience is built upon several core components:

Emotional Regulation: The ability to manage and respond to emotions effectively, maintaining composure and clarity in stressful situations.

Optimism: A positive outlook on life that fosters hope and motivation, even in the face of difficulties.

Adaptability: The capacity to adjust to new circumstances and changes, demonstrating flexibility and resourcefulness.

Self-Efficacy: A belief in one's own ability to influence outcomes and achieve goals, despite obstacles and setbacks.

Social Support: The presence of a strong support network of friends, family, and colleagues who provide encouragement and assistance during challenging times.

The Importance of Resilience

1. Enhances Mental Health

Resilience plays a crucial role in mental health by helping individuals cope with stress and adversity. It reduces the risk of developing mental health issues such as anxiety and depression and promotes overall psychological well-being. Resilient individuals are better equipped to manage their emotions and maintain a positive outlook, even in difficult situations.

2. Improves Physical Health

Resilience is linked to better physical health outcomes. Individuals with high resilience are more likely to engage in healthy behaviors, manage stress effectively, and recover more quickly from illness or injury. The ability to cope with stress and maintain a balanced perspective contributes to overall physical well-being.

3. Fosters Personal Growth

Building resilience contributes to personal growth and development. Facing and overcoming challenges can lead to increased self-awareness, confidence, and a sense of accomplishment. Resilient individuals often emerge from adversity with a deeper understanding of themselves and their capabilities.

4. Strengthens Relationships

Resilience enhances relationships by fostering effective communication, empathy, and support. Resilient individuals are better equipped to handle conflicts and maintain positive connections with others. A strong support network contributes to resilience and provides valuable resources during difficult times.

Strategies for Building Resilience

1. Develop Emotional Awareness

Practice Self-Reflection: Take time to reflect on your emotional experiences and responses. Journaling, meditation, or talking with a therapist can help you gain insight into your emotions and identify patterns.

Identify Triggers: Recognize the situations or events that trigger emotional stress. Understanding your triggers allows you to develop strategies for managing your reactions.

2. Cultivate a Positive Mindset

Practice Gratitude: Regularly acknowledge and appreciate the positive aspects of your life. Keeping a gratitude journal or expressing thanks to others can shift your focus from challenges to positive experiences.

Reframe Negative Thoughts: Challenge and reframe negative thoughts by considering alternative perspectives or focusing on potential solutions. Cognitive restructuring helps you maintain a more balanced and optimistic outlook.

3. Build Strong Social Connections

Foster Relationships: Cultivate and maintain strong relationships with family, friends, and colleagues. Engage in activities that strengthen your connections and provide mutual support.

Seek Support: Don't hesitate to reach out for help when needed. Whether through friends, family, or professional resources, seeking support can provide valuable assistance and perspective during challenging times.

4. Develop Problem-Solving Skills

Break Down Challenges: When faced with a problem, break it down into smaller, manageable steps. Identify possible solutions and create a plan of action.

- Learn from Experiences: Reflect on past challenges and the strategies that helped you overcome them. Use these experiences to inform your approach to current and future obstacles.

5. Enhance Adaptability

Embrace Change: Approach change with an open mind and a willingness to adapt. Flexibility and resilience are closely related, and being open to new possibilities can help you navigate transitions more effectively.

Develop New Skills: Continuously seek opportunities for personal and professional growth. Learning new skills and expanding your knowledge can enhance your ability to adapt to changing circumstances.

6. Practice Self-Care

Prioritize Well-Being: Engage in activities that promote physical, emotional, and mental well-being. Exercise, healthy eating, and sufficient sleep are fundamental to maintaining resilience.

Engage in Relaxation Techniques: Incorporate relaxation techniques such as deep breathing, mindfulness, or yoga into your routine. These practices help manage stress and maintain emotional balance.

7. Set Realistic Goals

Establish Achievable Objectives: Set clear, realistic goals that align with your values and aspirations. Break down larger goals into smaller, actionable steps to maintain motivation and track progress.

Celebrate Progress: Recognize and celebrate your achievements, no matter how small. Celebrating milestones reinforces your sense of accomplishment and motivation.

8. Learn from Setbacks

View Failures as Opportunities: Approach setbacks as opportunities for learning and growth. Reflect on what you can learn from challenges and how you can apply these lessons in the future.

Maintain Persistence: Stay committed to your goals and continue making progress despite setbacks. Persistence and determination are key components of resilience.

Building Resilience in Specific Contexts

1. In the Workplace

Foster a Supportive Environment: Create a work environment that supports resilience by encouraging open communication, providing resources for stress management, and promoting a healthy work-life balance.

Develop Leadership Skills: Leaders can enhance resilience within their teams by modeling adaptive behaviors, offering support, and providing opportunities for growth and development.

2. In Personal Relationships

Practice Effective Communication: Build resilience in personal relationships by communicating openly, listening actively, and resolving conflicts constructively.

Offer Support: Provide support and encouragement to loved ones during challenging times. Strengthening relationships through mutual support fosters resilience and emotional well-being.

3. In Facing Health Challenges

Adopt a Positive Attitude: Maintain a positive attitude and focus on aspects of your health that you can control. Engage in activities that promote well-being and seek support from healthcare professionals and loved ones.

Utilize Coping Strategies: Develop coping strategies to manage the emotional and physical aspects of health challenges. Practices such as relaxation techniques, support groups, and self-care can enhance resilience.

Conclusion:

Building resilience is a journey of personal growth and self-discovery. By developing emotional awareness, cultivating a positive mindset, building strong social connections, and enhancing adaptability, you can strengthen your capacity to navigate life's challenges with grace and strength. Resilience is not a fixed trait but a dynamic quality that can be nurtured and developed over time.

Embrace the process of building resilience with patience and perseverance, and recognize that each challenge is an opportunity for growth and learning. By fostering resilience, you can navigate adversity with greater ease, maintain emotional balance, and achieve a deeper sense of fulfillment and well-being. Through resilience, you not only overcome obstacles but also unlock your full potential and create a life of strength and purpose.

Chapter 9: Enhancing Self-Confidence

Enhancing Self-Confidence: A Journey to Empowerment

Introduction:

Self-confidence is the cornerstone of personal growth and success. It empowers individuals to pursue their goals, overcome challenges, and embrace their true potential. Building self-confidence is not about having an inflated sense of self-importance but about developing a genuine belief in your abilities and worth. This chapter explores the essence of self-confidence, its significance, and practical strategies for enhancing it, guiding you on a transformative journey toward empowerment and self-assurance.

Understanding Self-Confidence

1. Defining Self-Confidence

Self-confidence is the belief in one's abilities, qualities, and judgment. It involves having a positive yet realistic view of oneself and one's potential. Confident individuals trust their skills and decisions, enabling them to take risks, face challenges, and pursue their aspirations with assurance.

2. The Components of Self-Confidence

Self-confidence encompasses several key components:

Self-Efficacy: Belief in one's ability to accomplish specific tasks or goals.

Self-Esteem: A general sense of self-worth and value.

Self-Acceptance: Embracing and accepting oneself, including strengths and weaknesses.

Resilience: The ability to recover from setbacks and maintain confidence in the face of adversity.

3. The Role of Self-Confidence

Self-confidence plays a crucial role in various aspects of life:

Personal Growth: It encourages you to step outside your comfort zone, try new things, and pursue personal development.

Career Success: Confidence enhances performance, helps in seizing opportunities, and contributes to career advancement.

Relationships: Confident individuals build healthier and more fulfilling relationships through effective communication and self-assurance.

Decision-Making: Confidence enables you to make decisions with clarity and conviction, leading to more effective problem-solving.

The Benefits of Enhancing Self-Confidence

1. Improved Performance

Self-confidence boosts performance by enhancing focus, motivation, and perseverance. When you believe in your abilities, you are more likely to take proactive steps toward achieving your goals and overcoming obstacles.

2. Greater Resilience Confident individuals are better equipped to handle setbacks and challenges. They view failures as opportunities for growth rather than as reflections of their inadequacies, maintaining a positive outlook and continuing to move forward.

3. Enhanced Relationships

Self-confidence fosters healthier relationships by promoting open communication, setting boundaries, and expressing needs and desires. Confident individuals are more likely to engage in meaningful interactions and build strong connections with others.

4. Increased Opportunities

Confidence opens doors to new opportunities and experiences. It encourages you to take risks, seek out new challenges, and pursue your passions with enthusiasm and determination.

Strategies for Enhancing Self-Confidence

1. Set Realistic Goals

Define Clear Objectives: Establish specific, achievable goals that align with your values and aspirations. Break down larger goals into smaller, manageable steps to maintain motivation and track progress.

Celebrate Milestones: Acknowledge and celebrate your achievements, no matter how small. Recognizing your progress reinforces your sense of accomplishment and boosts confidence.

2. Develop Self-Awareness

Reflect on Strengths: Take time to identify and reflect on your strengths, talents, and accomplishments. Acknowledge your achievements and how they contribute to your self-confidence.

Embrace Self-Reflection: Engage in regular self-reflection to understand your thoughts, feelings, and behaviors. Journaling or mindfulness practices can help you gain insight and build self-awareness.

3. Practice Positive Self-Talk

Challenge Negative Thoughts: Identify and challenge negative or self-doubting thoughts. Replace them with positive affirmations that reinforce your abilities and potential.

Affirmations: Use positive affirmations to build self-confidence. Repeating statements such as "I am capable" or "I am worthy" can help shift your mindset and boost self-belief.

4. Develop Competence and Skills

Pursue Learning Opportunities: Invest in developing new skills and knowledge that enhance your competence and expertise. Continuous learning and growth contribute to greater self-confidence.

Seek Feedback: Solicit constructive feedback from trusted sources to gain insight into your strengths and areas for improvement. Use feedback as a tool for growth and self-improvement.

5. Practice Self-Care

Prioritize Well-Being: Engage in activities that promote physical, emotional, and mental well-being. Regular exercise, healthy eating, and sufficient rest contribute to a positive self-image and increased confidence.

Engage in Relaxation Techniques: Incorporate relaxation practices such as deep breathing, meditation, or yoga into your routine. These techniques help manage stress and maintain a balanced perspective.

6. Build Supportive Relationships

Surround Yourself with Positivity: Cultivate relationships with people who support and uplift you. Positive social connections provide encouragement and reinforce your self-confidence.

Seek Mentorship: Find mentors or role models who inspire you and provide guidance. Learning from their experiences and insights can boost your confidence and help you navigate challenges.

7. Embrace Challenges and Take Risks

Step Outside Your Comfort Zone: Embrace opportunities to challenge yourself and take risks. Facing new experiences and overcoming fears build resilience and self-confidence.

Learn from Failures: View setbacks as learning experiences rather than as failures. Reflect on what you can learn from challenges and use those insights to grow and improve.

8. Practice Gratitude and Self-Compassion

Acknowledge Achievements: Regularly express gratitude for your accomplishments and experiences. Recognizing your successes and efforts fosters a positive self-image.

Be Kind to Yourself: Practice self-compassion by treating yourself with kindness and understanding. Avoid self-criticism and recognize that everyone makes mistakes and experiences setbacks.

Overcoming Common Obstacles to Self-Confidence

1. Dealing with Self-Doubt

Identify the Source: Reflect on the underlying causes of self-doubt and address them directly. Understanding the root of your doubts allows you to challenge and overcome them.

Reframe Perspectives: Shift your focus from perceived weaknesses to strengths and achievements. Reframe self-doubt as an opportunity for growth and learning.

2. Handling Criticism

Separate Criticism from Self-Worth: Understand that criticism is not a reflection of your value as a person. Focus on constructive feedback and use it to improve rather than internalize negative judgments.

Respond Constructively: Approach criticism with an open mind and a willingness to learn. Respond to feedback positively and use it to enhance your skills and confidence.

3. Managing Perfectionism

Set Realistic Standards: Recognize that perfection is an unattainable ideal. Set realistic and achievable goals that allow for growth and improvement without excessive self-imposed pressure.

Embrace Imperfection: Accept that mistakes and imperfections are part of the learning process. Focus on progress and growth rather than striving for unattainable perfection.

Enhancing Self-Confidence in Different Areas of Life

1. In the Workplace

Take Initiative: Volunteer for new projects or responsibilities to demonstrate your abilities and build confidence in your professional skills.

Seek Professional Development: Pursue opportunities for training and development to enhance your expertise and boost your confidence in your career.

2. In Personal Relationships

Communicate Effectively: Practice assertive communication to express your needs and desires clearly. Confidence in expressing yourself strengthens relationships and fosters mutual respect.

Set Boundaries: Establish and maintain healthy boundaries in relationships. Confidently setting boundaries demonstrates self-respect and fosters positive interactions.

3. In Pursuing Hobbies and Interests

Explore New Interests: Take up new hobbies or interests that align with your passions and strengths. Engaging in activities you enjoy builds confidence and a sense of fulfillment.

Share Your Talents: Share your skills and talents with others through hobbies or community involvement. Contributing your abilities fosters self-assurance and positive feedback.

Conclusion:

Enhancing self-confidence is a transformative journey that empowers you to embrace your true potential and navigate life's challenges with assurance. By setting realistic goals, developing self-awareness, practicing positive self-talk, and nurturing supportive relationships, you can cultivate a genuine belief in your abilities and worth.

Self-confidence enriches various aspects of life, including personal growth, career success, and relationships. It allows you to face challenges with resilience, seize opportunities with enthusiasm, and build meaningful connections with others.

Embrace the journey of enhancing self-confidence with patience and perseverance. Recognize and celebrate your achievements, practice self-compassion, and remain open to growth and learning. Through your efforts, you not only build self-confidence but also unlock the path to empowerment, fulfillment, and a more enriched and meaningful life.

Chapter 10: Cultivating Positive Relationships

Cultivating Positive Relationships: The Art of Connection

Introduction:

Human relationships are the cornerstone of our emotional and social well-being. Cultivating positive relationships involves more than simply interacting with others; it requires intentional effort to build trust, understanding, and mutual respect. Positive relationships enhance our lives, providing support, joy, and a sense of belonging. This chapter explores the principles of cultivating positive relationships, the benefits they offer, and practical strategies for nurturing meaningful connections with others.

The Foundations of Positive Relationships

1. Trust

Trust is the bedrock of any positive relationship. It involves believing in the reliability, integrity, and competence of others. Trust fosters openness and honesty, creating a safe environment where individuals feel valued and supported.

2. Respect

Respect involves acknowledging and valuing the individuality and perspectives of others. It includes treating people with kindness, recognizing their boundaries, and appreciating their unique qualities. Respect is fundamental to building strong, enduring connections.

3. Empathy

Empathy is the ability to understand and share the feelings of others. It involves putting yourself in someone else's shoes, listening actively, and responding with compassion. Empathy strengthens bonds by fostering deeper emotional connections and mutual support.

4. Communication

Effective communication is crucial for cultivating positive relationships. It includes both verbal and non-verbal aspects, such as active listening, clear expression, and appropriate body language. Open and honest communication helps resolve conflicts, build trust, and enhance understanding.

The Benefits of Positive Relationships

1. Emotional Support

Positive relationships provide emotional support during times of stress, uncertainty, or hardship. Having a network of supportive individuals offers comfort, encouragement, and reassurance, helping you navigate challenges with greater resilience.

2. Increased Happiness

Engaging in positive relationships contributes to overall happiness and life satisfaction. Meaningful connections bring joy, companionship, and a sense of belonging, enhancing your overall well-being and quality of life.

3. Personal Growth

Positive relationships foster personal growth by providing feedback, encouragement, and diverse perspectives. They challenge you to reflect on your values, goals, and behaviors, supporting your development and self-improvement.

4. Enhanced Resilience

Strong relationships enhance resilience by offering a support system during difficult times. Knowing that you have people who care about you and are willing to help builds confidence and helps you face adversity with greater strength.

Strategies for Cultivating Positive Relationships

1. Practice Active Listening

Give Full Attention: When engaging in conversation, focus fully on the speaker. Avoid distractions, and show that you are listening through eye contact, nodding, and verbal affirmations.

Reflect and Clarify: Reflect on what the speaker has said and ask clarifying questions if needed. This demonstrates that you value their perspective and are genuinely interested in understanding their message.

Avoid Interruptions: Allow the speaker to finish their thoughts before responding. Interrupting can undermine effective communication and may hinder the development of a positive connection.

2. Show Appreciation and Gratitude

Express Thanks: Regularly express appreciation for the efforts, kindness, and support of others. Simple gestures, such as saying "thank you" or writing a note of appreciation, can strengthen relationships.

Acknowledge Achievements: Celebrate the accomplishments and milestones of those around you. Recognizing their successes fosters positive interactions and demonstrates your support.

3. Be Genuine and Authentic

Be Yourself: Authenticity fosters trust and deepens connections. Share your true thoughts, feelings, and experiences, and encourage others to do the same.

Honesty and Transparency: Communicate honestly and openly, even when discussing difficult topics. Transparency builds trust and ensures that relationships are grounded in truth.

4. Respect Boundaries

Understand Limits: Recognize and respect the personal boundaries of others. Avoid pressuring or intruding on their private space or decisions.

Communicate Needs: Clearly communicate your own boundaries and needs, and be receptive to the boundaries set by others. Mutual respect for boundaries fosters healthy and respectful relationships.

5. Practice Empathy

Validate Feelings: Acknowledge and validate the emotions and experiences of others. Show that you understand and appreciate their feelings, even if you have a different perspective.

Offer Support: Provide support and encouragement when others are facing challenges. Empathy involves being present and offering help when needed, demonstrating your care and concern.

6. Resolve Conflicts Constructively

Address Issues Early: Address conflicts and misunderstandings as soon as they arise. Avoid letting issues fester, as unresolved conflicts can damage relationships.

Use "I" Statements: Express your feelings and concerns using "I" statements to avoid placing blame. For example, say "I feel concerned when..." instead of "You always..." to communicate your perspective more effectively.

Seek Solutions Together: Collaboratively work towards solutions that satisfy both parties. Focus on finding common ground and reaching agreements that respect the needs and feelings of everyone involved.

7. Invest Time and Effort

Prioritize Relationships: Make time for meaningful interactions with the people you care about. Prioritizing relationships demonstrates your commitment and investment in building positive connections.

Engage in Shared Activities: Participate in activities and experiences that you both enjoy. Shared experiences strengthen bonds and create lasting memories.

8. Encourage Growth and Development

Support Goals: Encourage and support the personal and professional goals of others. Offer guidance, resources, and encouragement to help them achieve their aspirations.

Provide Constructive Feedback: Offer feedback that is supportive and constructive. Help others identify areas for growth and development in a positive and encouraging manner.

Building Positive Relationships in Different Contexts

1. In the Workplace

Foster Collaboration: Promote a collaborative work environment by encouraging teamwork, sharing knowledge, and supporting colleagues. Building positive relationships at work enhances productivity and job satisfaction.

Recognize Contributions: Acknowledge the efforts and achievements of your coworkers. Recognition fosters a positive work culture and motivates individuals to perform at their best.

2. In Personal Relationships

Create Quality Time: Spend quality time with family and friends, engaging in activities that strengthen your connection. Prioritize meaningful interactions and shared experiences.

Navigate Challenges Together: Address challenges and conflicts in personal relationships with empathy and understanding. Work together to find solutions and strengthen your bond.

3. In Community Involvement

Engage in Volunteer Work: Participate in community service or volunteer activities to connect with others and contribute to a greater cause. Building relationships through shared values and goals fosters a sense of community and belonging.

Support Local Initiatives: Support and participate in local events, organizations, or initiatives. Engaging with your community strengthens relationships and enhances your connection to the broader social fabric.

Conclusion:

Cultivating positive relationships is an ongoing journey that enriches our lives and contributes to our overall well-being. By practicing active listening, showing appreciation, being genuine, respecting boundaries, and fostering empathy, you can build and nurture meaningful connections with others.

Positive relationships provide emotional support, enhance happiness, and foster personal growth. Investing time and effort into building and maintaining these connections is a valuable endeavor that leads to a more fulfilling and balanced life.

Embrace the art of cultivating positive relationships with intention and care. Through your efforts, you create a network of support, understanding, and joy that enhances your life and the lives of those around you. In building positive relationships, you not only create a sense of belonging but also contribute to a world of kindness, respect, and shared growth.

Chapter 11: Mastering Communication Skills

Mastering Communication Skills: The Key to Effective Connection

Introduction:

Communication is the cornerstone of human interaction, influencing every relationship, whether personal or professional. It's more than just the exchange of words; it's the way we connect, understand, and influence each other. Mastering communication skills is essential for building strong relationships, resolving conflicts, and achieving success in every aspect of life. This chapter will explore the art of effective communication, offering practical tips and strategies to help you express yourself clearly, listen actively, and connect deeply with others.

The Importance of Communication Skills

Effective communication is a powerful tool that can transform your life. Here's why mastering communication skills is crucial:

Builds Strong Relationships: Clear and open communication fosters trust, understanding, and empathy, which are the foundations of strong, lasting relationships.

Enhances Career Success: Whether you're leading a team, negotiating a deal, or collaborating with colleagues, effective communication is key to professional success.

Resolves Conflicts: Good communication helps prevent misunderstandings and allows for constructive conflict resolution, leading to healthier, more harmonious relationships.

Influences and Persuades: The ability to articulate your thoughts and ideas clearly allows you to influence others, inspire action, and achieve your goals.

Boosts Confidence: Mastering communication skills boosts your self-confidence, enabling you to express yourself assertively and handle challenging situations with ease.

The Elements of Effective Communication

Effective communication involves several key elements that work together to ensure that your message is understood and received as intended:

1. Clarity

- Clarity is the foundation of effective communication. It involves expressing your thoughts, ideas, and emotions in a straightforward and unambiguous manner. To communicate clearly, avoid jargon, use simple language, and be concise. Ensure that your message is easy to understand and free from unnecessary complexity.

2. Active Listening

- Communication is a two-way process, and listening is just as important as speaking. Active listening involves fully concentrating on the speaker, understanding their message, and responding thoughtfully. It requires you to be present, avoid interrupting, and show genuine interest in what the other person is saying.

3. Nonverbal Communication

- Nonverbal cues, such as body language, facial expressions, eye contact, and tone of voice, play a significant role in communication. They often convey more than words alone. Be mindful of your nonverbal signals, as they can reinforce or contradict your spoken message. Similarly, pay attention to the nonverbal cues of others to gain a deeper understanding of their feelings and intentions.

4. Empathy

- Empathy is the ability to understand and share the feelings of another person. It's a crucial component of effective communication, as it allows you to connect with others on an emotional level. Practice empathy by putting yourself in the other person's shoes, acknowledging their emotions, and responding with compassion and understanding.

5. Feedback

- Providing and receiving feedback is essential for clear communication. When giving feedback, be constructive, specific, and respectful. When receiving feedback, be open-minded, listen without becoming defensive, and use the feedback as an opportunity for growth and improvement.

6. Adaptability

- Different situations and audiences require different communication styles. Being adaptable means adjusting your communication approach to suit the context and the needs of the listener. Whether you're speaking to a large audience, having a one-on-one conversation, or communicating in writing, tailor your message to ensure it resonates with your audience.

Strategies for Mastering Communication Skills

Now that we've explored the key elements of communication, let's delve into practical strategies to help you master these skills:

1. Practice Active Listening

- Active listening is more than just hearing the words being spoken. It involves fully engaging with the speaker, both mentally and emotionally. To practice active listening, focus on the speaker without distractions, acknowledge their message with nods or verbal affirmations, and ask questions to clarify your understanding. Reflecting back what the speaker has said in your own words can also demonstrate that you've understood their message.

2. Enhance Your Nonverbal Communication

- Your body language, facial expressions, and tone of voice are powerful tools in communication. Make eye contact to show interest, use open body language to convey approachability, and vary your tone of voice to emphasize key points. Be aware of any unconscious habits, such as crossing your arms or avoiding eye contact, that might send the wrong message.

3. Be Clear and Concise

- When communicating, especially in a professional setting, clarity and brevity are key. Organize your thoughts before speaking, and focus on the main points you want to convey. Avoid unnecessary details or tangents that could confuse your listener. Remember, it's not about saying a lot; it's about saying what matters.

4. Develop Emotional Intelligence

- Emotional intelligence (EI) is the ability to recognize, understand, and manage your own emotions, as well as those of others. High EI enhances your communication skills by allowing you to navigate social situations with sensitivity and awareness. To develop EI, practice self-awareness by reflecting on your emotional responses, manage your emotions in stressful situations, and show empathy toward others.

5. Ask Open-Ended Questions

- Open-ended questions encourage deeper conversations and provide the speaker with the opportunity to elaborate on their thoughts. Instead of asking questions that can be answered with a simple "yes" or "no," ask questions that begin with "how," "what," or "why." For example, "What do you think about this approach?" or "How did that experience make you feel?"

6. Provide Constructive Feedback

- Giving feedback is a vital communication skill, especially in leadership and collaborative roles. When providing feedback, focus on specific behaviors rather than personal attributes, and offer suggestions for improvement. Use the "sandwich" method: start with a positive comment, provide constructive criticism, and end with encouragement. This approach helps maintain a positive and productive dialogue.

7. Practice Empathy

- Empathy strengthens your connections with others and fosters a sense of understanding and trust. Practice empathy by actively listening to others, acknowledging their feelings, and responding with kindness and support. In difficult conversations, try to see the situation from the other person's perspective and consider how they might be feeling.

8. Be Mindful of Cultural Differences

- In our increasingly globalized world, it's important to be aware of cultural differences in communication styles. What is considered polite or appropriate in one culture may be perceived differently in another. Educate yourself about the cultural norms of your audience, and approach cross-cultural communication with sensitivity and respect.

9. Improve Your Written Communication

- Written communication is just as important as verbal communication, especially in professional settings. To improve your writing, focus on clarity, coherence, and tone. Use short paragraphs, bullet points, and headings to make your message easy to read. Always proofread your writing for grammar, spelling, and punctuation errors before sending.

10. Engage in Continuous Learning

- Communication is a skill that can always be improved. Seek opportunities to enhance your communication skills by attending workshops, reading books on the subject, and practicing in real-life situations. The more you practice, the more confident and effective you'll become as a communicator.

Overcoming Common Communication Challenges

Even with strong communication skills, challenges can arise. Here are some strategies for overcoming common communication barriers:

1. Managing Nervousness

- Nervousness can interfere with your ability to communicate effectively, especially in public speaking or high-stakes situations. To manage nervousness, practice deep breathing, prepare thoroughly, and focus on the message rather than the fear. Visualizing a positive outcome can also help reduce anxiety.

2. Dealing with Difficult Conversations

- Difficult conversations, whether they involve conflict or delivering bad news, require a delicate approach. Start by setting a positive tone, listen actively, and express your concerns with empathy and respect. Focus on finding a solution rather than assigning blame, and be open to compromise.

3. Handling Miscommunication

- Miscommunication can lead to misunderstandings and conflicts. To prevent miscommunication, clarify your message, ask for feedback, and summarize key points to ensure everyone is on the same page. If a miscommunication does occur, address it promptly and work together to resolve any issues.

Conclusion:

Mastering communication skills is a journey that requires practice, patience, and a commitment to personal growth. By developing clarity, active listening, empathy, and adaptability, you can enhance your ability to connect with others, resolve conflicts, and achieve your goals.

Effective communication is more than just exchanging words; it's about understanding and being understood. It's the key to building strong relationships, influencing others, and navigating the complexities of life with confidence and grace.

As you continue to refine your communication skills, you'll find that your ability to connect, inspire, and lead will flourish, opening doors to new opportunities and enriching every aspect of your life.

Embrace the power of communication, and watch as your relationships, career, and personal growth reach new heights.

Chapter 12:Unlocking Creativity and Innovation

Unlocking Creativity and Innovation: A Pathway to Boundless Possibilities

Introduction:

Creativity and innovation are the driving forces behind progress, whether in art, science, business, or daily life. They are the sparks that ignite new ideas, challenge conventional thinking, and lead to groundbreaking discoveries. Yet, many people believe that creativity is an elusive gift reserved for a select few. The truth is, creativity and innovation are not innate traits but skills that can be cultivated and nurtured. This chapter will guide you on a journey to unlock your creative potential and embrace innovation, empowering you to think differently, solve problems more effectively, and bring your unique vision to life.

Understanding Creativity and Innovation

Creativity is the ability to generate new, original ideas, while innovation involves applying those ideas to create something of value. These concepts are often intertwined, as innovation requires a creative mindset to identify opportunities and develop novel solutions. Whether you're an artist seeking inspiration, an entrepreneur looking to disrupt the market, or simply someone striving to think outside the box, unlocking creativity and innovation is essential for personal and professional growth.

The Myths of Creativity

Before diving into the techniques for unlocking creativity, it's important to dispel some common myths that may be holding you back:

Myth 1: Creativity is a natural talent.

- While some people may have a natural inclination toward creative thinking, creativity is a skill that anyone can develop. It's about learning to see the world differently and being open to new experiences.

Myth 2: Creativity only exists in the arts.

- Creativity is not limited to artistic endeavors. It can be applied to any field, from science and technology to business and education. Creativity is about solving problems and exploring new possibilities in any domain.

Myth 3: Creativity requires a lack of structure.

- While spontaneity can spark creativity, structure and discipline can also enhance it. Setting constraints and working within boundaries can actually stimulate creative thinking by challenging you to find innovative solutions.

Myth 4: Innovation is only for inventors and entrepreneurs.

- Innovation is not confined to inventors or entrepreneurs. It's a mindset that anyone can adopt, whether you're looking to improve processes at work, develop new products, or find better ways to manage your daily life.

Techniques for Unlocking Creativity

Now that we've addressed the myths, let's explore practical techniques to unlock your creativity and foster innovation:

1. Cultivate Curiosity

- Curiosity is the foundation of creativity. It's the desire to explore, ask questions, and seek out new experiences. Cultivate curiosity by exposing yourself to different perspectives, learning about new subjects, and being open to the unknown. The more curious you are, the more creative ideas you'll generate.

2. Embrace Divergent Thinking

- Divergent thinking is the process of generating multiple ideas or solutions to a problem. It encourages you to think broadly and consider a wide range of possibilities. Practice divergent thinking by brainstorming without judgment, allowing your mind to wander, and exploring unconventional approaches. Remember, there are no bad ideas in the creative process—only opportunities for exploration.

3. Create a Creative Environment

- Your environment plays a significant role in your ability to think creatively. Surround yourself with inspiration, whether it's art, nature, books, or people who challenge and inspire you. Create a space that encourages creative thinking by reducing distractions, adding elements of nature, and keeping tools for creativity—such as notebooks, sketchpads, or whiteboards—within reach.

4. Engage in Play

- Play is a powerful tool for unlocking creativity. It allows you to explore ideas without pressure or constraints. Engage in activities that are fun, lighthearted, and unrelated to your work, such as playing games, doodling, or improvising. Playfulness stimulates the brain, encourages experimentation, and leads to unexpected insights.

5. Practice Mindfulness

- Mindfulness involves being fully present in the moment and aware of your thoughts and feelings without judgment. By practicing mindfulness, you can quiet the inner critic that often stifles creativity and allow your mind to flow freely. Techniques such as meditation, deep breathing, and mindful observation can help you tap into your creative potential.

6. Seek Inspiration from Others

- Creativity doesn't happen in a vacuum. Seek inspiration from others by collaborating with diverse groups, attending workshops or conferences, and studying the work of creative individuals in your field. Exposure to different ideas and perspectives can spark new insights and fuel your creativity.

7. Challenge Assumptions

- Innovation often arises from challenging the status quo. Question the assumptions and norms that govern your thinking and look for ways to disrupt them. Ask "What if?" and "Why not?" to explore new possibilities. By challenging assumptions, you can break free from conventional thinking and discover innovative solutions.

8. Embrace Failure

- Failure is an inevitable part of the creative process. Rather than fearing failure, embrace it as a learning opportunity. Each failure brings you closer to finding a solution that works. Adopt a growth mindset, where mistakes are seen as valuable lessons, and keep experimenting until you achieve your desired outcome.

9. Practice Creative Problem-Solving

- Creative problem-solving involves approaching challenges with an open mind and exploring multiple solutions. Use techniques such as mind mapping, reverse brainstorming, or the SCAMPER method (Substitute, Combine, Adapt, Modify, Put to another use, Eliminate, Rearrange) to generate creative solutions. The key is to stay flexible and willing to explore unconventional ideas.

10. Take Breaks and Disconnect

- Sometimes, the best way to unlock creativity is to step away from the problem. Taking breaks, especially spending time in nature, allows your mind to rest and reset. Disconnecting from screens and routine activities can create the mental space needed for creative insights to emerge.

Fostering Innovation in Your Life and Work

Once you've unlocked your creativity, the next step is to channel it into innovation. Here are some strategies to help you foster innovation in your personal and professional life:

1. Adopt a Growth Mindset

- A growth mindset is the belief that abilities and intelligence can be developed through effort, learning, and persistence. Embrace challenges, learn from feedback, and view obstacles as opportunities for growth. A growth mindset fosters a culture of innovation by encouraging experimentation and continuous improvement.

2. Encourage Collaboration

- Innovation thrives in collaborative environments where diverse ideas and perspectives come together. Foster a culture of collaboration by encouraging open communication, cross-disciplinary teamwork, and brainstorming sessions. Collaboration amplifies creativity and leads to more innovative solutions.

3. Experiment and Prototype

- Innovation requires a willingness to experiment and test ideas. Develop a mindset of experimentation by creating prototypes or minimum viable products (MVPs) to test your ideas quickly and gather feedback. Iterating on your ideas based on real-world feedback helps you refine and improve your innovations.

4. Stay Agile and Adaptable

- The ability to adapt to change is crucial for innovation. Stay agile by being open to new information, pivoting when necessary, and continuously iterating on your ideas. Flexibility and adaptability allow you to respond to evolving circumstances and seize new opportunities.

5. Celebrate Creative Successes

- Recognize and celebrate creative successes, both big and small. Celebrating achievements reinforces the value of creativity and innovation and motivates you and your team to continue pushing boundaries. Create a culture that values and rewards creative thinking and innovation.

Conclusion:

Unlocking creativity and innovation is not a one-time event but an ongoing journey of exploration, experimentation, and growth. By cultivating curiosity, embracing divergent thinking, challenging assumptions, and fostering collaboration, you can tap into your creative potential and drive innovation in all areas of your life.

Remember, creativity and innovation are within everyone's reach. They are not limited by profession, age, or experience. The more you practice and nurture these skills, the more they will flourish, leading to boundless possibilities and a life rich with new ideas, solutions, and opportunities.

Embrace the journey of unlocking creativity and innovation, and watch as your life and work are transformed by the power of original thinking and the courage to explore the unknown.

Chapter 13: Creating a Balanced Life

Creating a Balanced Life: The Path to Harmony and Fulfillment

Introduction:

In a world marked by constant demands and rapid changes, achieving a balanced life can seem elusive. However, creating a balanced life is essential for fostering well-being, joy, and a sense of fulfillment. A balanced life integrates various aspects of our existence, including work, relationships, health, and personal growth, harmonizing them to create a satisfying and purposeful experience. This chapter explores the concept of a balanced life, its importance, and practical strategies for achieving and maintaining equilibrium across different areas of life.

Understanding a Balanced Life

1. Defining Balance

A balanced life is one where different areas of your life are in harmony, each receiving appropriate attention and care. It involves achieving a state of equilibrium where work, relationships, health, and personal growth are aligned and supported, leading to overall satisfaction and well-being.

2. The Dimensions of a Balanced Life

Work: Managing career responsibilities and aspirations in a way that aligns with personal values and goals.

Relationships: Nurturing meaningful connections with family, friends, and partners.

Health: Prioritizing physical, mental, and emotional well-being through healthy habits and self-care.

Personal Growth: Investing in self-improvement, learning, and personal development.

3. The Benefits of a Balanced Life

Enhanced Well-Being: Balance fosters physical, mental, and emotional health, leading to greater overall well-being.

Reduced Stress: Equilibrium among various life aspects helps prevent burnout and manage stress effectively.

Increased Fulfillment: A balanced life promotes satisfaction and contentment by aligning daily activities with personal values and goals.

Improved Relationships: Balance enhances the quality of relationships by ensuring time and attention are dedicated to nurturing connections.

Strategies for Creating a Balanced Life

1. Define Your Priorities

Identify Core Values: Reflect on what is most important to you in life. Identifying your core values helps guide decisions and actions, ensuring that they align with your vision of balance.

Set Clear Goals: Establish specific, achievable goals in different areas of your life. Clear goals provide direction and motivation, helping you allocate time and resources effectively.

2. Create a Well-Structured Routine

Develop a Daily Schedule: Create a daily routine that allocates time for work, relationships, health, and personal growth. A structured schedule helps manage time effectively and maintain balance.

Incorporate Flexibility: Allow for flexibility in your routine to adapt to unexpected events and changes. Balance involves being adaptable while staying true to your priorities.

3. Manage Your Time Effectively

Use Time Management Tools: Employ tools such as calendars, planners, and time-tracking apps to organize and manage your activities. Effective time management helps allocate appropriate time to each area of your life.

Prioritize Tasks: Prioritize tasks based on their importance and urgency. Focus on high-priority activities and delegate or postpone less critical tasks.

4. Nurture Relationships

Invest in Quality Time: Spend meaningful time with family, friends, and partners. Prioritize activities that strengthen your connections and foster positive interactions.

Communicate Openly: Practice effective communication to build trust and understanding in your relationships. Open and honest conversations contribute to stronger and more fulfilling connections.

5. Prioritize Health and Well-Being

Adopt Healthy Habits: Incorporate regular exercise, balanced nutrition, and adequate rest into your routine. Healthy habits support physical well-being and overall balance.

Practice Self-Care: Engage in activities that promote mental and emotional health, such as relaxation techniques, hobbies, and mindfulness practices. Self-care helps maintain equilibrium and manage stress.

6. Invest in Personal Growth

Pursue Learning Opportunities: Engage in continuous learning and self-improvement. Personal growth contributes to a sense of purpose and fulfillment.

Set Personal Development Goals: Establish goals for personal growth, such as acquiring new skills, pursuing interests, or engaging in creative pursuits. Personal development enhances self-awareness and confidence.

7. Create Boundaries

Set Work-Life Boundaries: Establish clear boundaries between work and personal life. Avoid overworking and ensure that time is allocated for relaxation and personal activities.

Respect Personal Boundaries: Communicate and respect the boundaries of others. Healthy boundaries in relationships contribute to balance and mutual respect.

8. Embrace Flexibility and Adaptability

Be Open to Change: Embrace changes and adjustments as part of the journey to balance. Flexibility allows you to adapt to new circumstances and maintain equilibrium.

Reevaluate and Adjust: Regularly assess your balance and make adjustments as needed. Life is dynamic, and periodic reevaluation helps ensure that you remain aligned with your priorities and goals.

Balancing Different Areas of Life

1. Work-Life Balance

Create a Balanced Work Schedule: Ensure that your work schedule allows for sufficient time for personal activities, relaxation, and family. Avoid excessive overtime and prioritize work-life harmony.

Seek Professional Growth: Pursue career development opportunities that align with your values and goals. Balance involves achieving professional success while maintaining personal well-being.

2. Balancing Relationships

Foster Quality Connections: Invest time and energy into building and maintaining meaningful relationships. Balance involves nurturing connections with loved ones while also making time for individual pursuits.

Address Relationship Needs: Communicate and address the needs and expectations of your relationships. Balance requires active engagement and mutual understanding.

3. Balancing Health and Wellness

Integrate Physical Activity: Incorporate regular physical activity into your routine. Exercise promotes physical health and contributes to overall balance.

Maintain Mental and Emotional Health: Prioritize mental and emotional well-being through self-care practices, relaxation techniques, and seeking support when needed.

4. Balancing Personal Growth Pursue Passion Projects: Engage in activities and projects that align with your interests and passions. Personal growth involves exploring and nurturing your talents and creativity.

Set Development Goals: Establish goals for personal growth and development. Balance involves continuous learning and self-improvement while managing other life responsibilities.

Overcoming Challenges to Balance

1. Managing Overcommitment

Learn to Say No: Set boundaries and decline additional commitments that may disrupt your balance. Prioritize existing responsibilities and avoid overextending yourself.

Delegate and Share Responsibilities: Share tasks and responsibilities with others when possible. Delegating helps manage workload and maintain balance.

2. Addressing Stress and Burnout

Identify Stressors: Recognize sources of stress and address them proactively. Managing stress effectively contributes to maintaining balance and well-being.

Practice Stress-Reduction Techniques: Incorporate stress-reduction techniques such as mindfulness, deep breathing, and relaxation exercises into your routine.

3. Navigating Life Transitions

Adapt to Change: Embrace life transitions and changes with a flexible mindset. Adjusting to new circumstances requires adapting your approach to maintaining balance.

Seek Support: Reach out for support from friends, family, or professionals during times of transition. Support systems help navigate change and maintain equilibrium.

Conclusion:

Creating a balanced life is an ongoing journey that involves harmonizing various aspects of your existence to achieve a fulfilling and meaningful experience. By defining your priorities, establishing a well-structured routine, managing time effectively, nurturing relationships, prioritizing health, investing in personal growth, and embracing flexibility, you can cultivate a sense of balance and well-being.

A balanced life promotes overall satisfaction, reduces stress, and enhances relationships. Embrace the principles of balance with intention and commitment, and remain open to adapting as life evolves. Through mindful efforts and a holistic approach, you create a life of harmony, fulfillment, and lasting joy.

Chapter 14: Physical Health and Wellness

Physical Health and Wellness: The Foundation of a Vibrant Life

Introduction:

Physical health and wellness are the cornerstones of a fulfilling and vibrant life. They empower us to pursue our dreams, engage in meaningful activities, and enjoy the journey of life with energy and enthusiasm. Achieving and maintaining physical wellness involves more than just exercise and diet; it's about nurturing your body, mind, and spirit in harmony. This chapter will guide you through the essential aspects of physical health and wellness, offering insights and practical tips to help you live your healthiest life.

Understanding Physical Health and Wellness

Physical health refers to the well-being of your body and its ability to function optimally in daily life. Wellness, on the other hand, is a broader concept that encompasses not just physical health, but also mental, emotional, and spiritual well-being. Together, physical health and wellness create a balanced and holistic approach to living a healthy and satisfying life.

The Core Components of Physical Health

1. Nutrition

- Proper nutrition is the fuel that powers your body. A balanced diet, rich in whole foods such as fruits, vegetables, lean proteins, and whole grains, provides the essential nutrients your body needs to function at its best. Good nutrition supports everything from energy levels to immune function, mental clarity, and emotional stability.

2. Exercise and Physical Activity

- Regular physical activity is crucial for maintaining a healthy body. Exercise strengthens your muscles, improves cardiovascular health, boosts mental health, and enhances overall quality of life. Incorporating a variety of exercises—such as strength training, cardiovascular workouts, flexibility exercises, and mind-body practices like yoga—ensures a well-rounded fitness routine.

3. Sleep

- Sleep is the body's natural way of rejuvenating and healing. Quality sleep is essential for physical recovery, mental clarity, emotional balance, and overall well-being. Aim for 7-9 hours of sleep each night, and prioritize good sleep hygiene by creating a restful environment and establishing a consistent sleep routine.

4. Hydration

- Water is vital for every bodily function, from regulating temperature to aiding digestion and maintaining skin health. Staying adequately hydrated supports energy levels, cognitive function, and overall vitality. Aim to drink plenty of water throughout the day, adjusting your intake based on your activity level and environment.

5. Preventive Care

- Preventive care includes regular check-ups, screenings, and vaccinations to detect and prevent health issues before they become serious. Taking proactive steps to monitor your health—such as getting regular physical exams, dental check-ups, and eye exams—ensures that you catch potential problems early and maintain optimal health.

Cultivating a Lifestyle of Physical Wellness

Achieving physical health and wellness is not just about following strict routines or diets; it's about creating a sustainable lifestyle that you enjoy and that supports your overall well-being. Here are some key principles to help you cultivate a lifestyle of physical wellness:

1. Prioritize Movement

- Make physical activity a regular part of your day. Whether it's taking a brisk walk, dancing, swimming, or practicing yoga, find activities that you enjoy and that fit your lifestyle. Aim for at least 150 minutes of moderate aerobic activity or 75 minutes of vigorous activity each week, along with muscle-strengthening exercises on two or more days.

2. Eat Mindfully

- Mindful eating is about being present and intentional with your food choices. Pay attention to what you eat, how you eat, and why you eat. Choose foods that nourish your body, savor each bite, and listen to your body's hunger and fullness cues. This approach not only improves digestion but also enhances your relationship with food.

3. Listen to Your Body

- Your body communicates with you through sensations, emotions, and energy levels. Learn to listen to your body's signals—whether it's the need for rest, movement, nourishment, or hydration. Responding to these signals with care and compassion is key to maintaining balance and avoiding burnout.

4. Manage Stress

- Chronic stress can take a toll on your physical health, leading to issues such as headaches, digestive problems, and weakened immunity. Incorporate stress-reduction techniques into your daily routine, such as deep breathing, meditation, journaling, or spending time in nature. Prioritize activities that help you relax and recharge.

5. Build Healthy Habits

- Developing healthy habits is the foundation of lasting physical wellness. Start small by setting achievable goals, such as drinking more water, walking 10,000 steps a day, or reducing sugar intake. Gradually build on these habits over time, and celebrate your progress along the way.

6. Stay Consistent

- Consistency is key to maintaining physical health and wellness. While it's normal to have off days, strive to make healthy choices most of the time. Remember that wellness is a journey, not a destination, and that small, consistent actions lead to lasting change.

The Mind-Body Connection

Physical health is deeply interconnected with mental and emotional well-being. The mind-body connection emphasizes the importance of aligning your thoughts, emotions, and physical actions to achieve overall wellness.

1. Mental Fitness

- Just as you exercise your body, it's important to exercise your mind. Engage in activities that challenge and stimulate your brain, such as puzzles, reading, learning new skills, or practicing mindfulness. Mental fitness enhances cognitive function, emotional resilience, and overall quality of life.

2. Emotional Balance

- Emotions play a significant role in physical health. Chronic negative emotions, such as stress, anger, or sadness, can manifest as physical symptoms. Cultivate emotional balance by practicing self-awareness, expressing your feelings, and seeking support when needed. Positive emotions, such as joy, gratitude, and love, have a powerful impact on physical well-being.

3. Mindful Movement

- Mindful movement practices, such as yoga, tai chi, or pilates, combine physical exercise with mindfulness and breath awareness. These practices enhance flexibility, strength, and balance while also promoting relaxation and mental clarity. Incorporating mindful movement into your routine supports both physical and mental wellness.

Conclusion:

Physical health and wellness are the foundation upon which a vibrant, fulfilling life is built. By nourishing your body with wholesome foods, staying active, getting enough rest, and taking care of your mental and emotional well-being, you can create a lifestyle that supports long-term health and happiness.

Remember, the journey to physical wellness is a personal and ongoing process. It's about making choices that align with your unique needs and goals, and finding joy in the pursuit of a healthy, balanced life. With commitment, compassion, and consistency, you can achieve and maintain the physical health and wellness that empowers you to live your best life.

Chapter 15:Financial Well-being

Financial Well-being: A Path to Prosperity and Peace of Mind

Introduction:

In the journey of life, financial well-being is not merely about accumulating wealth; it is about achieving a harmonious balance between your income, expenses, and savings, all while aligning with your personal values and goals. True financial well-being encompasses both the tangible and intangible aspects of life—providing a sense of security, freedom, and the ability to live a life of purpose and fulfillment.

Understanding Financial Well-being

Financial well-being is a state of being where a person can fully meet their current and ongoing financial obligations, feel secure in their financial future, and make choices that allow them to enjoy life. It's not just about how much money you have, but how you manage it, the peace of mind it brings, and the ability to make decisions without financial stress.

The Four Pillars of Financial Well-being

1. Financial Security

- This pillar is about having a stable source of income and being able to cover your essential needs without worry. Financial security means having an emergency fund, insurance coverage, and a budget that allows you to live within your means. It's the foundation upon which all other financial well-being is built.

2. Financial Freedom

- Financial freedom is the ability to make life choices without being overly constrained by financial factors. It includes having the flexibility to pursue your passions, whether that means taking a career break, starting a new venture, or simply spending more time with loved ones. Financial freedom is achieved through smart investments, managing debt wisely, and planning for the future.

3. Financial Knowledge

- Knowledge is power, especially when it comes to finances. Understanding how money works—from basic budgeting to more complex investment strategies—is crucial for making informed decisions. Financial literacy empowers you to navigate the financial world confidently, avoid common pitfalls, and take advantage of opportunities that align with your goals.

4. Financial Purpose

- Having a clear financial purpose is about knowing what you want your money to achieve for you. Whether it's securing your family's future, giving back to your community, or achieving personal dreams, a strong sense of financial purpose guides your spending, saving, and investing decisions. It ensures that your financial actions are in harmony with your personal values.

Building Your Financial Well-being

Achieving financial well-being is a continuous process that involves planning, discipline, and ongoing education. Here are some steps to help you on your journey:

1. Set Clear Financial Goals

- Begin by identifying what financial success looks like for you. Your goals might include paying off debt, saving for retirement, purchasing a home, or creating a travel fund. Prioritize your goals and create a roadmap to achieve them.

2. Create a Budget

- A budget is the cornerstone of financial well-being. It provides a clear picture of your income, expenses, and savings, helping you to manage your money effectively. Track your spending, cut unnecessary expenses, and allocate funds toward your financial goals.

3. Build an Emergency Fund

- Life is unpredictable, and having an emergency fund can provide a safety net during unexpected events like medical emergencies or job loss. Aim to save at least three to six months' worth of living expenses in a readily accessible account.

4. Manage Debt Wisely

- Not all debt is bad, but managing it wisely is crucial. Prioritize paying off high-interest debt first, and consider consolidating or refinancing options to lower your interest rates. Avoid accumulating new debt unless it's for a well-planned investment.

5. Invest for the Future

- Investing is key to growing your wealth and achieving long-term financial goals. Diversify your investments across different asset classes, such as stocks, bonds, and real estate, to spread risk. Start early to take advantage of compound interest.

6. Protect Your Assets

- Insurance is a critical component of financial well-being. Protect yourself and your loved ones by ensuring you have adequate health, life, and property insurance. Review your policies regularly to make sure they still meet your needs.

7. Educate Yourself Continuously

- The financial world is constantly evolving, and staying informed is essential. Take advantage of resources like books, online courses, seminars, and financial advisors to continually expand your financial knowledge.

The Emotional Side of Financial Well-being

Financial well-being isn't just about numbers; it's also about your mindset and emotional relationship with money. Here's how you can cultivate a positive financial mindset:

1. Practice Gratitude

- Focus on what you have rather than what you lack. Gratitude shifts your perspective from scarcity to abundance, helping you appreciate your financial situation and make decisions from a place of contentment.

2. Avoid Comparison

- Comparing your financial situation to others can lead to dissatisfaction and poor financial decisions. Instead, focus on your own goals and progress. Remember, everyone's financial journey is unique.

3. Seek Balance

- Financial well-being is about balance—between saving and spending, work and leisure, security and freedom. Regularly assess your financial habits to ensure they align with your overall well-being and happiness.

4. Build a Support Network

- Surround yourself with people who support your financial goals and values. Whether it's a partner, family, or friends, having a network of like-minded individuals can provide encouragement and accountability.

Conclusion:

Financial well-being is a lifelong journey that goes beyond the mere accumulation of wealth. It's about making informed decisions, securing your financial future, and living a life of purpose and joy. By focusing on the four pillars of financial well-being—security, freedom, knowledge, and purpose—you can create a stable foundation for a prosperous and fulfilling life.

Remember, financial well-being is within your reach. With careful planning, continuous education, and a positive mindset, you can achieve the financial stability and freedom you desire, paving the way for a life rich in experiences, opportunities, and peace of mind.

Chapter 16: Digital Detox and Tech Management

Digital Detox and Tech Management: Reclaiming Balance in a Hyperconnected World

Introduction:

In our hyperconnected world, technology is both a blessing and a challenge. While it offers unprecedented convenience, connectivity, and access to information, it can also lead to overwhelm, distraction, and a sense of disconnection from the present moment. The concept of a digital detox—taking a deliberate break from technology—has gained popularity as a way to restore balance and enhance well-being. Tech management, on the other hand, involves creating healthy boundaries and practices to maintain a sustainable relationship with technology. This chapter will explore the importance of digital detox and tech management, offering practical tips and strategies to help you reclaim control over your digital life and find harmony in a tech-driven world.

The Impact of Technology on Well-being

Technology has revolutionized the way we live, work, and connect with others. However, its pervasive presence can also have negative effects on our mental, emotional, and physical well-being. Some common challenges associated with excessive tech use include:

Information Overload: The constant influx of information from emails, social media, news, and notifications can lead to cognitive overload, making it difficult to focus, process information, and make decisions.

Digital Burnout: Prolonged exposure to screens and constant connectivity can contribute to stress, anxiety, and burnout. The pressure to be "always on" can erode boundaries between work and personal life, leading to exhaustion.

Reduced Attention Span: The rapid pace of digital content, coupled with the temptation to multitask, can shorten attention spans and reduce our ability to concentrate on tasks for extended periods.

Sleep Disruption: The blue light emitted by screens interferes with the production of melatonin, the hormone that regulates sleep. Late-night screen time can disrupt sleep patterns, leading to poor sleep quality and daytime fatigue.

Social Disconnection: While technology enables virtual connections, it can sometimes detract from face-to-face interactions and the deep, meaningful connections that are essential for emotional well-being.

Recognizing these challenges is the first step toward creating a healthier relationship with technology. A digital detox allows us to step back, reset, and reconnect with ourselves and the world around us.

What is a Digital Detox?

A digital detox involves taking a break from digital devices, including smartphones, computers, tablets, and televisions. The goal is to reduce reliance on technology, minimize distractions, and create space for activities that promote mindfulness, creativity, and connection with others.

A digital detox can take many forms, from a few hours of tech-free time each day to a full weekend or even a week without screens. The key is to design a detox that aligns with your lifestyle and goals.

The Benefits of a Digital Detox

Taking a break from technology can have profound benefits for your well-being:

Increased Mindfulness: Disconnecting from digital distractions allows you to be more present in the moment, enhancing your awareness of your thoughts, feelings, and surroundings.

Improved Focus and Productivity: A digital detox can help you regain your ability to concentrate on tasks without the constant pull of notifications and social media. This can lead to increased productivity and a greater sense of accomplishment.

Enhanced Creativity: Stepping away from screens creates mental space for creativity to flourish. Without the constant input of information, your mind is free to explore new ideas and solutions.

Better Sleep: Reducing screen time, especially before bed, can improve your sleep quality by allowing your body to produce melatonin naturally. This leads to more restful sleep and greater energy during the day.

Deeper Connections: A digital detox can strengthen your relationships by encouraging more meaningful, face-to-face interactions. It allows you to connect with others without the distraction of devices.

Practical Strategies for a Successful Digital Detox

Embarking on a digital detox doesn't have to be daunting. Here are some practical strategies to help you get started:

1. Set Clear Intentions

- Before starting your digital detox, take some time to reflect on your goals. Are you looking to reduce stress, improve focus, or deepen your relationships? Clarifying your intentions will help you stay committed to the process and make the most of your detox experience.

2. Choose a Timeframe

- Decide how long you want your digital detox to last. It could be a few hours each day, a weekend, or even a full week. Choose a timeframe that feels achievable and fits with your schedule. You can gradually increase the duration of your detox as you become more comfortable with the process.

3. Inform Others

- Let friends, family, and colleagues know that you're doing a digital detox. This will help them understand why you may be less responsive to messages and encourage them to support your efforts. You might even inspire others to join you!

4. Create Tech-Free Zones

- Designate specific areas of your home as tech-free zones. For example, you might choose to keep your bedroom, dining room, or living room free from screens. This creates physical spaces where you can relax, unwind, and connect with others without the distraction of devices.

5. Schedule Screen-Free Activities

- Plan activities that don't involve screens to fill your detox time. Consider reading a book, going for a walk, practicing yoga, cooking a meal, journaling, or spending quality time with loved ones. Engaging in these activities can help you rediscover the joys of offline life.

6. Use Technology Mindfully

- During your detox, practice using technology mindfully. When you do need to use a device, be intentional about it. Avoid multitasking, and focus on one task at a time. This will help you maintain a balanced relationship with technology even after your detox ends.

7. Reflect on the Experience

- After your digital detox, take some time to reflect on how you felt during the process. Did you notice any changes in your mood, focus, or energy levels? What did you learn about your relationship with technology? Use these insights to guide your future tech habits.

Tech Management: Creating Sustainable Digital Habits

A digital detox is a powerful reset, but sustainable tech management is key to maintaining a healthy relationship with technology in the long term. Here are some strategies to help you manage your tech use effectively:

1. Set Boundaries

- Establish clear boundaries around your tech use. For example, you might decide to check emails only during certain hours, limit social media to 30 minutes a day, or turn off notifications during specific times. Setting boundaries helps you regain control over your time and attention.

2. Prioritize Human Interaction

- Make a conscious effort to prioritize face-to-face interactions over digital communication. Whether it's spending time with family, catching up with friends, or participating in community activities, these interactions are vital for emotional well-being and can't be replaced by online connections.

3. Practice Digital Minimalism

- Digital minimalism is the practice of simplifying your digital life by focusing only on the essential tools and platforms that add value to your life. Declutter your digital environment by unsubscribing from unnecessary emails, unfollowing accounts that don't inspire you, and deleting apps that you rarely use.

4. Use Technology to Support Well-being

- Leverage technology to enhance your well-being rather than detract from it. Use apps that promote mindfulness, track your physical activity, or help you manage stress. By being intentional with your tech use, you can harness its benefits without falling into the trap of overuse.

5. Take Regular Digital Breaks

- Incorporate regular digital breaks into your daily routine. Even short breaks, such as stepping away from your screen for a few minutes each hour, can help reduce eye strain, boost productivity, and refresh your mind.

6. Engage in Offline Hobbies

- Cultivate hobbies and activities that don't involve screens. Whether it's gardening, painting, playing a musical instrument, or hiking, these activities provide a welcome break from technology and contribute to your overall well-being.

Conclusion:

In a world where technology is an integral part of daily life, a digital detox and effective tech management are essential for maintaining balance and well-being. By taking deliberate breaks from screens, setting boundaries, and using technology mindfully, you can reclaim control over your digital life and create space for the things that truly matter.

Remember, the goal is not to eliminate technology entirely but to cultivate a healthy, intentional relationship with it. By integrating these practices into your life, you can enjoy the benefits of technology while protecting your mental, emotional, and physical health.

Embrace the journey of digital detox and tech management, and discover the freedom, clarity, and connection that come from living a more balanced life.

Final Reflections and Next Steps

The Journey of Personal Mastery

As we reach the final chapter of this book, it's time to reflect on the transformative journey you've undertaken. From building self-awareness to mastering communication skills, you've delved into the essence of what it means to live a fulfilled and balanced life. Every chapter has been a step toward unlocking your full potential, a guide to navigating the complexities of personal growth, and a companion on your path to self-mastery.

This journey hasn't just been about acquiring knowledge—it's about internalizing and applying that knowledge to create real change in your life. You've learned how to set goals that resonate with your true self, overcome procrastination, and cultivate resilience in the face of adversity. You've discovered the power of emotional intelligence, the art of managing your time with precision, and the importance of building strong, positive relationships. Each of these elements is a piece of the puzzle that, when assembled, forms a complete picture of a life well-lived.

But remember, the process of self-help and personal development is ongoing. The insights you've gained are not static—they are dynamic tools that will evolve with you as you continue to grow. Life will present new challenges and opportunities, and with the skills you've honed, you'll be equipped to face them with confidence and grace.

Think of this book not as a conclusion, but as a beginning—a launchpad into the next chapter of your life. You are now armed with the knowledge and strategies to live intentionally, to push beyond your limits, and to create a life that is not only successful but also deeply meaningful.

As you close this book, take a moment to appreciate how far you've come. The thirst for growth, the desire for improvement, and the quest for balance that brought you here have all been quenched with the wisdom contained within these pages. But the journey of personal mastery is never truly over. It's an ever-evolving adventure, one that promises continued discovery, joy, and fulfillment.

So, step forward with confidence. Embrace the life that awaits you with an open heart and a determined spirit. The tools are now in your hands, and the world is full of possibilities. Your story is still being written, and the best is yet to come.

A request to my loving readers

Give your valuable feedback for improvement of the book.

contact me
email-sprashant.tukun@gmail.com

www.ingramcontent.com/pod-product-compliance
Lightning Source LLC
Chambersburg PA
CBHW080243170726
48282CB00031B/1183
* 9 7 8 9 3 3 4 1 2 4 2 9 3 *